how
to
make
herself
agreeable
to
everyone

RANDOM HOUSE · NEW YORK

how
to
make
herself
agreeable
to
everyone

cameron russell

Published in the United States by Random House, an imprint and division of Penguin Random House LLC, New York.

RANDOM HOUSE and the HOUSE colophon are registered trademarks of Penguin Random House LLC.

Library of Congress Cataloging-in-Publication Data
Names: Russell, Cameron, author.
Title: How to make herself agreeable to everyone: a memoir / Cameron Russell.
Description: First edition. | New York: Random House, [2024]
Identifiers: LCCN 2023035479 (print) | LCCN 2023035480 (ebook) |
ISBN 9780593595480 (hardcover) | ISBN 9780593595497 (ebook)
Subjects: LCSH: Russell, Cameron, 1987– | Models (Persons)—United
States—Biography | Models (Persons)—Psychology. | Clothing
trade—Moral and ethical aspects.
Classification: LCC HD8039.M772 U574 2024 (print) | LCC HD8039.M772 (ebook) |
DDC 746.9/2092 [B]—dc23/eng/20231220
LC record available at https://lccn.loc.gov/2023035479
LC ebook record available at https://lccn.loc.gov/2023035480

Printed in the United States of America on acid-free paper

randomhousebooks.com

9 8 7 6 5 4 3 2 1

First Edition

Book design by Debbie Glasserman

To my mother, Robin Chase

part
one

she'll do anything

1. On my first shoot the stylist says to his assistant: Let's go for
an S-N-M vibe. Mom, do you remember? I go to the toilet
and call you and say, They want to put a belt around my
neck, it's an S-N-M vibe, and you say no belt around my
neck, S *and* M is a sexual fetish. So I say no to the belt, and
he thinks I'm ungrateful.

By way of explanation I say: I want to run for president.
I have to be careful about the kind of pictures I take. He
looks me in the eye and I look back. Normally adults are
pleased or amused when I tell them this. But he rolls his
eyes and takes off the belt. He gives me a tiny black bikini.
Go! he says, and turns his back.

I've never worn a bikini before. I didn't know I would be
wearing one, but I don't have enough pubic hair yet to need
to shave. On set I suck my stomach in until my ribs poke

out. How do I stand when my stomach is showing? The photographer keeps telling me, Relax. He has a fart-machine prank he does. I laugh because I'm supposed to.

When the photo comes out, my agent makes it my comp card and sends it to clients. I carry it around to castings to give out. Your body looks amazing, she says.

The stylist won't work with me for another seven years. When he finally books me again, he jokes: You were such a spoiled brat.

2. On my second shoot the makeup artist paints my lips red, and in the mirror of the RV bathroom my teeth look stained next to the bright color. She tells me I have cocksucker lips. The stylist says I'm going to be huge.

3. My fourth or fifth shoot, the photographer—a legend— kisses me on the lips when I'm standing at the elevators waiting to leave. I am sixteen and the double kiss everyone does is awkward, and so I think maybe I messed it up. A dozen shoots and fifteen years later he will still call me "girl" when we work together and pretend he does not know my name.

4. The photographer adjusts my hair and clothes by placing his whole hand—heavy, warm—on my face, my shoulder, my hip, and then drawing it slowly back from my skin. He stands behind me in the mirror and looks at me and I look away and he squeezes my shoulders. Electricity shoots through me and I think about this feeling even after the shoot is over, when I'm back home, for weeks and months.

The agents keep telling me how much money I can make, but all I want is to experience this feeling again.

It turns out this shoot launches my career. A famous art director visits the set that day and says, Fuck, she's sexy, to the photographer. I try to be polite and make uncomfortable eye contact while they talk about how I look. Then, since I don't know what to say, I walk away and sink into a couch on the other side of the studio. I can still hear them looking through the images on the computer: Fuck, fuck, fuck, they say.

5. The next time we shoot he will ask me to shoot topless. But I'm sixteen, I say. I feel like I might cry. It has to be topless, says the stylist. I text you, Mom, and my new agent. The photographer asks me if I'm okay. I'm going to leave, I say, even though I don't want to, I just want to shoot with him wearing a top. I hug and double kiss him goodbye and walk out. Like we're breaking up. Of course, nobody cares; they have six other girls on set, ready to go.

6. The famous art director will nickname me "Camarones." He makes me lie in the dirt next to a swampy river, my body fake wet, sticky with baby oil, and tells me to arch my back and close my eyes. I stay lying in the mud, wondering if there are leeches, because they want my legs to stay where they are (positioned just so, spread at the water's edge) while the crew looks through Polaroids. The art director will come over and take pictures on his personal camera. Fuck, he says.

Mostly, though, they shoot their contract girl. At the

end of the first day the sky turns dark and the wind picks up and they turn a big spotlight on her lying in the reeds, wearing just jeans. The air is thick and wet. She is glowing. She covers her breasts with one arm and rolls around looking into the camera. Her lips get an extra spray from the makeup artist's glycerin bottle; they open. She is dripping. The rest of us disappear into the evening drizzle. When they are done, an assistant brings her a white robe, which she ties loosely. The art director throws an arm around her, the robe bunches, and I see her nipple. They walk together to a car, which will take them back to the hotel. Production shepherds me into the van with the rest of the crew.

The next day they shoot me again in the afternoon. God, you're sexy, says the art director. I don't know what to say. I wish I could have heard what their contract girl said when she was on set, but I couldn't get close enough.

7. I shoot a fragrance campaign with this same art director, and nobody tells me that I am the star of the campaign. Instead I sit alone for a day while everyone else shoots, wondering if I haven't made the cut. The second day he tells me, We need you making out with a guy. He suggests a model who is loud and obnoxious. I point and suggest another model whose name I don't know. It's just acting, I think. He laughs and says okay. So my first kiss is standing in a pool in underwear and a tank top. We kiss over and over for the cameras.

8. At castings—where the only time I get to speak is when I say, Good, thank you, after they ask, How are you today?— I get called purebred, all-American, well-educated, from a good family, maybe perfect for a contract, timeless, classic, but a little exotic, almost a little ethnic, do you have any Native American ancestry, the whole package, a triple threat. I'm still in high school, can't really sing or dance, and the last time I acted was in fourth grade, so I sense that what they mean is, I have the body, the face, and the White* skin they're looking for.

The walls at castings are covered with photos of nearly identical-looking White girls, for the summer season with tans, paler for fall/winter and couture. I am White, hip 33, waist 21, bust 33, 5' 9.5" but we could round up.

9. An art director who owns the magazine we're shooting for in Paris looks through the back of the RV while I change. At first I don't notice. He convinces my agent to have me take Polaroids with him. He asks me to go topless, I say no. *Chérie,* he says, this is Paris. But I want to run for president of the United States, I say. I can't take topless pictures.

I wonder if the reason why I've been saying I'm going to be president all these years is because I want to be treated like someone who might be president one day.

He shrugs, leaves the room, and returns with a strapless bra. When he shoots, one of his hands holds the camera and the other reaches to pull the top down.

Is it twisted? I ask.

Just need to hold it straight, he says. Eyes here, he says. The Polaroids fall onto the floor while he takes them.

---

*I capitalize "White" because it reminds me of how we name. Because it calls to mind an ugly, self-righteous centering as well as mortality, temporality. And I follow work by Dr. Nell Irvin Painter, who argued, "We should capitalize White to situate Whiteness within the American ideology of race, within which Black, but not White, has been hypervisible as a group identity. Both identities are products of the American ideology of race."

When he's done I look down and my nipples are exposed. How did I not feel the elastic sliding so low? The pictures develop and I see he has made me look topless.

As soon as I'm in the stairwell I feel my face get hot and tears roll down my cheeks. The whole thing happened too fast. I feel weak and stupid.

Dad picks me up from the airport when I get home, and I try to tell him about it.

Couldn't you have just said no? he asks.

I tried but the agency thought it was important.

I guess you'll know for next time.

When the magazine comes out, he's put me on the cover.

10. Next time is a decade later, when he requests me for a shoot and I waver while my agent convinces me, yes, I should do it. You need good editorial, she says. Okay. The shoot takes two days and the photos are fine. He treats me like an old friend and I act like one.

11. Photographers call me jailbait. One invites me to drinks. Eventually, I find my body in a bed next to him. Not myself: A lot of myself will be surprisingly gone by then. (You don't know how much of a self you are until you aren't.)

12. A French agent takes me out to dinner at a sushi restaurant where you can text other tables. Lots of men are there and they start texting our table. The agent brought his cousin too, and they are laughing, replying for me in French I don't understand. He takes me home on his motorcycle and I have to hold on tight to his body to be safe.

The agent gives his cousin my number and his cousin texts me asking if I'll go on a date with him. I say no—his cousin must be at least thirty and he lives in Paris and I didn't like him at dinner—but I save his number and his name in my phone, because I'm seventeen and nobody has ever asked me out before.

My French agent sends me emails and says he's in love. He says all the boys must be in love with me but I should go for a Frenchie. I try to respond like an adult, with sarcasm and distance. "You need a hobby," I write. Other emails I ignore, because what do you say?

13. My agent tells me they aren't shooting me because I'm a virgin.

14. My agent tells me they aren't shooting me because I lost my virginity.

15. During a night shoot the photographer keeps telling me, I want the in-between moment, not pose-y. Get into it, touch the guy. The male model, he means. Finally he gets a frame he likes where I am adjusting my dress and looking off camera. See, he says, showing me the shot, see here, it looks like you just got fucked.

16. I get my period in a white bikini on a beach when the whole crew is cis men. One of them asks if I cut myself. Blood runs down my leg and soaks through the white robe they gave me, and I have to wait to drive back to the hotel to get a tampon. I have to change in the photographer's bungalow room because this is where we are doing hair and makeup

and styling. The bathroom does not have a door, just a wall that divides it from the rest of the room, where the crew is sitting, passing a joint. Everyone is chilling. I am acting chill too, but the stylist asks me to remove my thong to wear a swimsuit they like, and I have to stay standing completely naked in the middle of the room while they untangle the swimsuit. I look at the floor. I do not know if the crew or the photographer are looking at me, or if I did a good enough job hiding my tampon string.

The photographer has me lie in the ocean at 5:00 A.M. as the sun rises, and I feel sick to my stomach, cramps, the water feels cold, and I am angry with myself for being spoiled.

17. I have enough money to buy an apartment and pay for college every semester. I have enough money that one day at the supermarket I realize I don't need to tally the groceries as I shop.

18. My agent tells me I need to sleep at the photographer's apartment in London because he cannot afford a hotel. Don't worry, she tells me, he's gay.

Years later the same photographer will ask me to change swimsuits on the beach in front of his assistants. When I say, No, I want a changing tent, he asks me, in front of everyone during lunch, Were you raped as a child? Is that why you're so sensitive?

19. The stylist puts me in a sheer shirt. I ask to wear a bra, and she says they don't have one. I ask the photographer to promise to retouch my nipples because, I tell him, I never

shoot topless or with nipples showing. He says, Of course. The pictures are published unretouched. When I email him, he says he remembers our agreement but it just didn't work artistically.

20. Okay, *mami* there, the photographer says. You really look Latin to me, he says. Normally I go for blonds, blond everywhere. He winks. Yes, lean there, touch your lips, hip out, yes. Like that. Legs crossed. Sometimes I think I could be straight, you know.

Oh yeah?

I mean, could you date a girl?

Sure, I say.

Yeah, me too. I'd be with ▮▮▮▮. Not just 'cause she's the super of all supers. Not just because we are really good friends. The thing is, this girl is amazing. She'll do anything. She's perfect. She's so sexy, she's the ultimate, you know?

Yeah, she's gorgeous.

The next morning the hairdresser will tell me the reason why ▮▮▮▮▮▮ is so amazing is because she'll do anything. Anything. The highest praise for a model. She's just nineteen but she gets it, he says. The new story they shot with her is out and everyone is looking through it.

Finally, we shoot the cover. You won't look like this forever, the photographer says, waving at my body. He lets the camera down and takes a step back. You really should let me shoot you naked. I love your body. When we've got the shot, everyone claps. I thank the photographer. We walk back to base camp together. He puts his arm around my waist. I'm so glad my first ▮▮▮▮▮▮ cover was with you, I say, and lean my head on his shoulder.

does the baby have dimples?

1.

Tolerate, synonym: swallow. A choice the body makes with the brain. How can I tell you that with every fiber of my being I participated? I worry I will break your heart. If I consented then I am not virtuous.

Why am I writing to you, Mom?

Your parental instinct is to ensure my survival, and you believe that depends on me being likable, employable, confident, and composed. So in order to tell you something we've never spoken about, because it would possibly undermine our carefully constructed exterior, while still reassuring you I will survive, I have to write a book to you. One that I can publish, and sell.

When I read Kiese Laymon's memoir *Heavy* addressed to his mother—"I am writing a different book to you because . . . I am afraid of speaking any of this to your face"—and Ocean Vuong's auto-fiction *On Earth We're Briefly Gorgeous*—"Dear Ma, I am writing to reach you—even if each word I put down is one word further from where you are"—I wonder whether this might be an American thing: We can't say to our mothers what we can't say publicly.

Since I never talk about modeling, my memories aren't organized into the right story yet. I'm going to start over, and it wouldn't make sense to call you *she,* because back then the story was still ours and you were still telling me how to make sense of things.

2.

Dad might be dying, Uncle Mark calls to tell you. So you and I go to Florida to be with your father.

It's hot. Grandpa's dog Beebee is walking around the house stinking like rotting flesh. You tell me, It's coming from his ears.

The hospital room where Grandpa is lying smells too, but not like anything I recognize. Everything there is just a little inhumane: two degrees too cold, walls too beige, doctor's teeth too dirty, machines making too many noises, and Dad—of course you call him Dad—too close to death.

We spent the first night sleeping next to him. When he's lucid he asks to go home. He wants to look at the ocean. He wants to be in his bed. You whisper to him, Hi, Dad, and you stroke his hand. His eyes are closed and wet, so you wipe them with a tissue. You wipe the corners of his mouth. He makes a move toward the tubes in his nose. You hold both his hands. They say we can't move you right now. You sit close to him, caressing him, speaking to him in a voice I haven't heard since my sister was born.

They wheel in a narrow cot for us. I make the bed with the hospital-provided sheet and the long red wool skirt that Grandma had thrown in the blanket bag, because we have piled everything else on Grandpa. We sleep without moving. We sleep so close our bones are touching.

In the morning we leave in the rental car. It's twenty minutes on the highway to your parents' house. We roll the windows down—the humidity and the wind feel like the only living things—and you start to tell me how you were raped for a year by the babysitter when you were two. Anal rape. I am looking at you but your eyes are on the road. Your hands are on the wheel. I cannot think of a way to be with you, and there is nothing worse than having you be alone. I want to feel everything you feel. I want to feel this for you, instead of you. I am the tough one. But all I can do is listen.

It's not something I share, you say.

Okay, I say.

I've told your dad, of course, and a couple of my close friends. My parents didn't report it; it was a different time. We were guests in Morocco and who knows what would have happened to him. He could have been put to death. My mom didn't even tell me about it, but then when I was nine I started having dreams, and when I told her about them she admitted they were true. My family would tease me, calling him my boyfriend.

That's awful.

It's so you understand. I don't want you to feel bad.

And then after a pause you half smile and say, I did a good job not telling you, huh? Not raising you to hate men.

I think I do.

Yes, but at least I didn't tell you to think that.

I look straight out the window, letting the dense forest blur, the road and the white line blur, four continuous brushstrokes, black-white-black-green, and then after a while, I move my eyes forward and let the trees linger long enough to take shape.

In case Grandpa gets better and comes home, you go around the house emptying all the alcohol down the drain. You find bottles under the sink and say, I think that's the last of it, and give me a bag to put out in the recycling.

We aren't there when he dies; my grandma and aunt are with him. We are at the movies watching *Pirates of the Caribbean* when your sister texts you. I ask if you want to leave but you say, Stay, it's almost over, so we sit still and hold hands watching Johnny Depp dance around a beach. On the way home we drive by the hospital because we left the neighbor's Scrabble set in Grandpa's room. You send me up to get it and they ask, Do you want to go in and see him? and I say, No, I just need to pick up the Scrabble. So a nurse goes in and gets it for me.

The next morning we drive Grandma to Pier 1 Imports. She wants a chair to replace Grandpa's chair. He always sat in the kitchen, in the best seat in the house, looking out toward the ocean with a breeze coming in off the water. His favorite line from any book ever was when the Rat said to the Mole in *The Wind in the Willows*, "Believe me, my young friend, there is *nothing*—absolute nothing—half so much worth doing as simply messing about in boats." But his chair is uncomfortable for her and when you offer, she agrees, yes, it would be nice to replace it, but she can keep his footstool. It's an errand on your to-do list. You want to make the house as nice for her as possible before we leave. She nods at the floor when you suggest going, and that's when you pick up on the uncomfortable timing of replacing the chair less than twelve hours after Grandpa passed.

She picks a large wicker chair from the outdoor furniture section, which is cheaper, but still expensive, eighty-five dollars new. I've never seen you buy much new, and certainly not furniture. Out in the parking lot we realize the trunk won't close over the new chair, even with the back seat down.

You say if I lie in the trunk we can keep it open and I can hold on to a leg to make sure the chair doesn't fly out. Dad's not here to figure out another way.

What if I fly out? I say.

I won't go too fast. Let's try it.

So I get in and you put the chair in after me and we drive off. It's hot in the trunk, but you're right, I don't fly out. It's a little scary to watch the highway, so I turn my head and look at the inside of the car.

You okay back there? you ask. Obviously I'm okay because I'm still in the car, so you start to giggle.

Now I'm laughing too, imagining what other drivers must be thinking.

I'm fine! I shout over the rushing of cars and wind. Get us home!

And now Grandma is laughing. We can't believe what we are doing, hurtling down the highway with the trunk open and me lying diagonally to keep my legs in the car and keep a grip on this ridiculous chair. My arm is getting pins and needles and I laugh harder and we all are laughing so hard all the way home, and just when we are wiping our eyes and out of breath we start up again because I stumble when I step out of the trunk in the driveway, my legs half asleep, my face bright red from heat.

Alone upstairs getting dressed, I put on all black and look in the mirror. I look tiny. I never wear black. Kids don't wear black, you always tell me. The skirt is yours and the shirt is new. Is it the black that makes my skin and hair look so golden? Is it the light? I move to the mirror in the bathroom in case anyone walks in. The light is even better here. I can see my face. My lips look pouty. My dark eyes almost match the black. I squint and drop my chin. Are they cat eyes? My breasts, now visible, are the size of half tennis balls under this shirt. I wonder if I'm curvy. I turn sideways to check.

How sick to spend time thinking about how I look on the day of your dad's ceremony.

A month ago you caught me looking in the mirror in the bathroom at home and said to your friend who was visiting: What is it about teenage girls and mirrors? because you knew it would embarrass me and make me stop. That time I was just popping a pimple, though. Now I really can't help myself, because I've never seen this person and suddenly in black I think I might look like a movie star. It feels almost like I'm looking at a creature, not a human.

When I come down, you send me back upstairs to change. You put on all black? This is a celebration! Put on one of the galabias your grandma embroidered.

3.

Child sexual abuse is deeply traumatizing. It is also very early training in power-over, in victim and offender, in coercion, in silencing, and in adapting to violence and domination. This is training related to all systems of oppression and power-over social conditions.

—STACI HAINES, *The Politics of Trauma*

You tell me that when I was a baby I screamed bloody murder when you dropped me off with the babysitter. You had a job you were trying to keep, so you left anyway. The whole day you thought maybe I was being molested by the adult son in the house and maybe you should leave and come get me. Why else would I scream that way? You brought me back the next day. More screaming. You say: The sitter literally had to pry you off my body. Again you worried all day. This happened until the week was over and you had time to figure something else out. When you tell me the story, I feel the boundaries of my body dissolve. I wonder if it's memory or inheritance.

You say I was a bad toddler. You say we got into shouting matches. You regretted having children. Once you slapped me and I said, If I could read, I'd get a parenting book from the library and it would say you're not supposed to do that. Once you angrily grabbed my arm and you were shocked to find it so small and soft. A toddler arm.

You play me a cassette tape as evidence:

Cameron, what are you drawing?

This? My voice is gravelly, deep, and double the volume of yours. From yelling all the time, you say, nodding.

Paper rustles on the tape. And then my voice again: This is a picture of a house that's burning and the little boy in the house is dead already and the little girl is running away through a field but her arm is on fire and her other arm fell off.

Do they have parents? young-you asks toddler-me.

The parents were murdered already.

Was the terror and surprise in your voice also suffused with awe? Were you hoping that in these violent words, this ruthless storytelling, the worst of the world had met its match?

You tell me about the first time I said I wanted to be president. You picked me up from day care and we were walking home.

Why are those people sleeping there?

They don't have anywhere else to go.

Why?

Ronald Reagan.

Who's that?

He was the president.

Can they live with us?

No.

Why not?

We don't know them.

Is the president the most powerful person in the world?

Probably.

I want to be president when I grow up.

You could. You smile like we're sharing a secret.

4.

I float face down in the ocean, observing my body stunned by the cold, like watching an animal.

The tide is quick. The cousins are leaning over the edge now, adrenaline making them hop at the sight of the drop, hands wringing, shouts flapping in the wind.

We come here because Grandpa is from Maine and he

bought a small house with his sister on the island in June 1962. A place to retire, a home base, something they owned. They wrote a novel: *Infinite Summer*. It's still in a box somewhere. After a month, there was a fire. You were four. You woke up to shouts and had to jump from the top of the steps over flames into your dad's arms. The house burned to the ground. They didn't have insurance so that was it, until you brought us back during summer vacation and all the siblings and cousins got together and decided to rebuild.

I scratch my thigh on the barnacle-covered ladder and emerge at the top, blood mixing with salt water and running in rivulets down my leg. A woman is watching me. At low tide the loading dock drops eighteen feet down, twenty-five if you stand on the tallest piling. I dive off without pause.

When I climb back up again, she's waiting at the top and introduces herself with two business cards, hers and a friend's. She does casting for TV and movies and her friend is an agent. I think you could model or maybe act if you wanted, she says. I thank her and wrap the cards in my dry shirt.

In this performance, where I am so much tougher, braver, and faster than the boys—who despite their new teenage muscle step down from the pilings and pause before they jump, then rush up the ladder as fast as they can to escape the cold—she's seen prettiness.

To prove a point, I climb the tallest piling, give her a nod as she joins the line for the ferry, and then fling myself off, arms wide. The crowd for the afternoon boat watches, cameras out.

I float again but I am too distracted. On the ladder I am ashamed to have performed for her and for the tourists on the dock. My slender summer limbs, my lips puffy with salt, my body dripping, what a brave girl, what a strong girl. Briefly thrilling to be admired, at the price of diminishing: What a girl.*

5.

"He's the strongest man in the world."

"Man, yes," said Pippi, "but I am the strongest girl in the world, remember that."

—ASTRID LINDGREN, *Pippi Longstocking*

Once, in the middle of the story, Grandma stops and asks me: What was his name? You know, your mom's "boyfriend"? But you tell me it's probably because your family was so nonchalant about the abuse that you survived.

I think to stop ourselves from feeling violence in our bodies, we turn our memories into myths, we make meaning to fill in gaps.

If a girl wanted to be a protagonist, all she had to do was outwit and outrun the boys. Your dad made sure you read all the girl heroes: Nancy Drew, Nancy Blackett, George (Georgina) Kirrin, Pippi Longstocking, Laura Ingalls Wilder, Harriet the Spy. Did I miss any? In cities, plains, and prairies, abandoned houses, with snakes lying in wait, on boats, in late verdant summer evenings, amid westward expansion, colonization, subjugation, supremacy, fear, and violence, a White girl could be exceptional.

---

* See: Judith Butler, "Gender Is Burning: Questions of Appropriation and Subversion," describing "recognition at an expense."

When I am still small enough, I sit between your legs in the bath.

What's that? I ask.

A stretch mark from you.

What's that? A five-inch scar on your thigh you don't want me to touch.

Too sensitive, you say, swatting.

You were playing in the woods in Swaziland, running across a dead tree in a game of tag. You fell. A broken branch ripped through your thigh. A man working nearby heard your cry. He tied his shirt like a tourniquet and carried you all the way back home.

How far?

A mile, maybe more.

You like the water hot. I have to sit on the edge to cool off. You sink deeper.

In Jerusalem you lived in the Arab quarter and your parents sent you to Arab school. You were eight, but they put you with the kindergarteners because you didn't know how to write in Arabic yet. It was important, you say, because we represented the United States. You were always the well-behaved daughter of a diplomat.

Bombs went off all the time. Once so close that a window of the apartment shattered. Your parents were out, and left a phone number, but this wasn't anything to report.

After two years your dad started getting death threats. He was telling Washington things the Israeli government didn't like.

The worst thing you ever did was poop in the window well of a church when you were seven.

You had your first kiss when you were twelve.

Your dad got in a car crash. You were in the back seat (no seatbelt) and knocked out your front tooth. Two people in the other car were killed. Now you have a fake tooth. Look in the light, you say, can't you see the color is different?

Your favorite smell is jasmine because in Alexandria, Egypt, jasmine grew outside your bedroom window. The summer you spent in Alex you went out dancing after dinner at nightclubs with your boyfriend and his parents. You woke up late and went to the beach. One weekend you took a trip with friends: two boys, two girls. You were all teenagers. The boys had a gun and got drunk and wanted to have sex with you. You and your friend locked the bathroom door and hid in the tub until morning. The enamel would probably stop a bullet. You snuck out while they were still sleeping and hitchhiked home.

In Jeddah, after high school, you got a job working for Lockheed Martin, transcribing ten-digit numbers. The woman who worked with you got promoted, and when you told your dad, he said, Well, have you seen her chest?

When you got pregnant you didn't find out my sex; you said it was the only time I'd get to be without a gender. When the nurse said, It's a girl, for a few seconds you were disappointed. Then you got over it and gave me a boy's name.

You tell me: If it were any other time in history we'd both have died. If not right away, then you right away and me later, of infection.

When you call Grandma, the first thing she asks is: Does the baby have dimples? I do.

A few weeks later you look in the mirror and think: I look like Eleanor Roosevelt. It was the first time I thought I really looked awful and finally understood that word, "matronly," you say.

People say: How nice, three boys. And you say, Thank you. Even though it's two girls, one boy. You give us all bowl cuts.

When I look at photos and ask you, Why? you say, It's what you wanted. Or sometimes: So you wouldn't get raped.

Girls get white discharge in their underpants when they hit puberty, and it's natural. Nobody told you, so you spent a summer in the library researching, and decided you must have syphilis.

I admit to you that sometimes, when I hear boys talking about jerking off, I wish I were a boy and could jerk off and feel great anytime, just like that. You say: Some girls masturbate too.

But I don't mean like that, I say, not knowing what I mean.

In the tub your eyes close and your words stop. I fidget at the end under the tap, where I barely fit. Soon we change positions and go head to toe with our hips offset. I start telling you stories. You want me to be valuable, to know how to put others at ease, keep them engaged and entertained. Like Scheherazade, who told stories to stay her own execution and stop the massacre of other women by the sultan, who married at night and murdered at dawn, I know I can only be powerful if people are listening, and I must be powerful if I want to survive.

6.

The power of photographs, Susan Sontag argued, is that they "furnish evidence. Something we hear about, but doubt, seems proven when we're shown a photograph of it."[1] Good stories, like photographs, freeze meaning; they turn memory into memorized lines.

So I am fascinated by your scars, your stretch marks, your fake tooth, and your pointer finger where the nail grows in a ridge since you sliced it in two with a table saw, because they reveal memories beyond fossilized fact, alive, animated in your flesh. You let me rub your nail between my thumb and forefinger like a charm, but when I try to use my nail to explore its edge, you pull back, wringing your hand.

At your parents' house, just on the right as you enter, are framed photographs of your dad laughing with King Sobhuza of Swaziland, the longest-reigning monarch, shaking hands with Anwar Sadat, then president of Egypt, clippings of the Kennedys, various black-and-white photographs of parties with dignitaries whose names only your older sister remembers. A photo of five of the six kids lined up tallest to smallest, the girls in matching handsewn dresses, you with dimpled toddler legs emerging from a crinoline at the very end. Eventually, in front of these, preserved behind dollar-store plexiglass, Grandma will display my *Vogue* covers and an image from a rapidly fading newspaper of me walking in the Victoria's Secret show.

When I was eight, Grandma cut a picture from the newspaper of a teenage Bill Clinton meeting JFK and mailed it to me. In the photo they shake hands, lean toward each other, Clinton wears a half smile, and they appear almost equals. His presidency: preordained. I already knew I needed a politically viable story-of-self, and I wondered how I could meet a president and make sure there was a photograph of it.

A decade from now I will measure the distance from model to president. You can see it in pictures. It's the distance between Trump's hand and the small of a teenage model's back at the Elite Model Look competition, it's Marilyn Monroe's breasts to JFK's jaw as he leans in to speak in the only photo that exists of the two.

it's easier if you relax

1.

I sign up for an on-camera acting class advertised in the adult-learning digest. It's held in a windowless room behind a Shaw's supermarket, where we sit on worn-out office chairs placed in a circle. Just in case the business cards lead to an audition, I don't want to mess it up. I pay for it with babysitting money.

I am the only kid. The class starts at 7:30 P.M. and you or Dad have to drive me there every single Monday night for a month and a half and wait in the parking lot until I am done, because there is no easy bus access. During the last class the teacher films us reading lines for fake commercials and gives us the VHS recordings to take home. I try to look in the camera the way she taught us. Like you're looking at someone, she says. Like you're looking into their eyes when you look into the lens.

I make the call the day after the class finishes, and a man on the other line says, Kit's not here right now, can I take a message?

Oh, I say, okay. Don't worry about it, I'll call back tomorrow.

She's actually gone this week. May I ask who's calling?

Eventually I hang up, mortified that I called a modeling agency, got rescheduled, and that I might be silly enough to call again. But I mark my planner anyway and call back. When we talk, Kit asks me how old I am and how tall. Just turned fifteen, I say. Five foot six and a little bit. She tells me to call back next summer. I keep her business card in my planner. Next summer I'm 5' 9" and she asks how soon I can come to New York, and I say, Next week.

Her office is in a tall building in Midtown Manhattan. When we arrive, she's leaning out a window into the air shaft, smoking. She takes Polaroid pictures of me and turns my chin with her thumb. Clench your teeth, she says. Look in profile. She measures my hips, waist, and bust with a cloth measuring tape and checks my height against a yardstick nailed to the wall.

She speaks to you as if I'm not there: She's perfect for Ralph Lauren or even Versace when she's a bit older. Maybe Calvin Klein. I can see her getting a contract—a coveted multi-year deal that could turn a model into a supermodel and paid millions. Kate and Calvin Klein. Christy and Maybelline. Gisele and Victoria's Secret. During her pitch to you she occasionally squints at me and runs her hands through my hair, flipping it to one side, then the other, like a professional appraiser.

Afterward we share a sandwich and a Snapple in Union Square, and you remember that you recently met someone who worked at a famous modeling agency. Maybe he can give us some advice. We call and your acquaintance tells us to come by the agency today, before we leave the city.

A man at the table next to ours turns around and says he couldn't help overhearing our conversation. He is a photographer and he thinks I could be very successful. He looks at the business card from last summer and tells us, If that agency your friend works for will take her, that's the better one. And don't pay for anything.

The first thing they give us at the better agency is a model-registration form.

Stage name? We check no. Nudity? No. Sheer? No. Topless? No. Fur? No.

You nod as I write. Or do I nod as you write? I can't remember. We accept what they offer. They assign me an agent, Charlotte, and she reassures us: This is just the standard form we give to everyone. She sets up a test photo shoot for the next morning and prints out a piece of paper with the details.

Back outside you say a good rule would be to only take photographs that wouldn't be embarrassing on the cover of *Time* magazine, considering my political ambitions.

No matter where we go in Manhattan, from Canal Street to the steps of the Met, Audrey Hepburn and Marilyn Monroe are for sale. Posters, postcards, magnets, drawings, key chains. I point this out to you and you shrug. They're incredibly famous, you say.

The next morning at the address Charlotte gave us, the freight elevator walls are plastered with fashion magazines and an older man sits on a high-backed stool next to buttons and a large hand brake. We tell him our floor and he nods, then says to me, Kate Moss, and raps a photo on the wall with his knuckle. I am surprised he has any interest in the women in these pictures, or that he finds them in any way related to me. I look at the wall for what might be any last-minute pointers. The doors open.

In the loft, between the kitchen and the photographer's bed, a paper backdrop hangs from a metal rod and the floor is marked with tape. After we shake hands, she gives me a black tank top and bikini bottom to change into. I go into her bathroom and come out half dressed, pulling the shirt down, wondering if it's meant to be a very short dress. But no, she says: Don't stretch it, you look good.

When I stand on the mark she says: No smiling. I am not sure what expression to make in a photo if I am not smiling. She takes a shot. Then she stops and hands me a tube of clear lip gloss that is so sticky and awkward to apply she takes it back. Like this, she says, dabbing her finger across my mouth. Behind my back I try to wipe the sticky off my finger and onto my palm before it's time to shoot again. She goes back to her camera and says, Relax your forehead. Do something with your arms.

Open your lips, she says. Breathe.

I think about how to relax my gluey lips. I try putting my hands on my hips.

She squints at me. Try something else. Grab the shirt.

She comes back over and moves my fingers. It's difficult to loosen fingers in a way that lets someone else manipulate them. When she's done she says, Now stay, and she adjusts the drooping arm holes so the sides of my breasts are covered.

She takes a few more pictures and goes to look for another outfit.

While she's in her closet I say to you, Wouldn't it be fun to take pictures jumping on that huge bed?

You glare at me. Don't you dare suggest that.

After we leave, while I try to get the glue-gloss off, you say, Why on earth would you think it's a good idea to take pictures on a bed?

It looked fun to jump on. It was so big, like a trampoline. (At home, we all sleep on futons.) I know, it was rude to suggest jumping on a stranger's bed.

What? you say. It will look like you just had sex. I see I'm going to have to teach you what not to do. If you ever end up shooting without me, don't lie on a bed, don't arch your back, don't close your eyes, don't sit with your legs open. Those are things that will make it look like you've had sex.

I hope you didn't forget anything.

The next day we pick up my new portfolio from the agency.

All the agents hug and double kiss me. They say: Oh my god, honey, those photos. They look me up and down and squeeze my waist. Yesterday's photos are already printed and sit inside clear plastic pocket pages of a heavy, oversized portfolio I will bring to show people at castings.

She's everything, they say to you. She's the whole package. I think I am supposed to either not talk or say thank you. So I say it. I whisper it. I feel uneasy. Saying I'm gorgeous over and over seems also like a way of saying I am otherwise uninteresting. Of course, that is sort of true; I'm just a kid, and the only thing that matters about me to them is something completely out of my control, and without them, I'd only ever made five bucks an hour babysitting.

When we are finally alone, walking back uptown to Uncle Gary's foldout couch, we can't stop looking at the portfolio. We stop on the street three times. We are conspirators.

I imagine it's the same as finding oil in the backyard. To think: Maybe I'm going to be a millionaire, but also, I really shouldn't be selling this.

Less than a week after we get home, Charlotte calls and we're back for show castings with the whole family. We are too many for Uncle Gary's, so you decide we can stay at a cheap hotel in

Midtown. You and Dad in the bed, the three of us kids on the floor using blankets from the closet.

I don't sleep. Instead I lean over the cold air conditioner and rest my forehead on the window, blinking out dry air. Thousands of windows, streetlamps, and traffic lights flicker. Manhattan looks like the stars fell out of the sky.

I am thinking about an interview with Avril Lavigne I read in a magazine, one that I had intended to hide because you said teen magazines were trash, but you saw it in my room and gasped: You paid money for that?

In the story, the reporter met Avril in her hotel room. She was eating room-service sugar cereal and wearing a hotel robe. She's only nineteen and they're interviewing her. I think about what I could say if I were being interviewed. I could talk about imperialist foreign policy, the illegal war in Iraq, voter disenfranchisement, and they would put it in the pages of a women's magazine. I have a plan for David Letterman too. Your TV was loud enough I could hear his interviews when I was supposed to be asleep. Actresses were flashing their breasts. In case I ever make it onto the show, I figure I can get out of it by showing him my third nipple. Just scandalous and silly enough to distract him and the audience. A little pink-brown bump we both have under our right breast, and then back to politics.

After you and Dad and the kids catch the bus back home, I stay at the agency so I can go to a party where Charlotte wants me to make an appearance.

She said I needed new clothes, so between castings you bought me a blue spaghetti-strap dress from Club Monaco. I put it on in the agency bathroom and come out barefoot to an audience of agents. They brush my hair into a low ponytail and release a cloud of hairspray to capture flyaways. Charlotte brings out from under her desk magenta heels she bought me at Nine West. She doesn't have an invite, so she sends me with another agent.

The party is in a garden on the roof of a high-rise building. They offer us champagne when we walk in.

The agent leads me by the elbow to meet an important executive.

You're going to make him rich, she says, and grabs my cheek.

She's a gold mine, he says.

Afterward Charlotte calls to ask how it went.

She said that? Really?

Yes, and grabbed my cheek.

That's great. Maybe we really can get you a contract.

We've already talked through every modeling hypothetical, though we knew almost none. The cliché pitfalls—drugs, sex— are preposterous. I've never kissed anyone.

Secretly I'm curious.

Last year in Danica's mom's basement we drank root beer and Anthony dared me to whisper everyone's name in their ear.

You're a weirdo, I said, and started to do it. When I whispered *Anthony* in his ear, he fell over backward.

Oh my god, he said, do it again.

No, I said.

Then do it to Jonah.

I whispered *Jonah* in Jonah's ear. They stared at each other.

What?

Your voice is like Angelina Jolie, like all deep and stuff.

Since I was too tough to be humiliated, I rolled my eyes and said, I did your dumb dare, your turn. And then, while Anthony took his turn snorting Altoid mint dust, a thought occurred to me—if the boys thought such a boring and effortless act was compelling, I must have some magic power. Now, with Charlotte calling to say famous designers were ready to hire me for their runway shows, the idea resurfaced.

Charlotte is already backstage with a sixteen-year-old model from Brazil when we arrive, and she asks you, Since you're a mother, could you take her to the bathroom and teach her how to use a tampon? She has to wear a swimsuit. Thank God I don't have my period yet.

While you're gone, a makeup artist takes me to a folding chair and puts lotion on my face. The lead hairdresser is giving an interview behind us about how they aren't doing anything, how the look is completely natural. I try to remember everything he's saying. I can't wait to tell you later: He was giving an interview about nothing!

At the second show hair and makeup takes three hours. They use multiple blow-dryers and I can't hear the conversation the hairdressers are having while they work on my head, so I sit with nothing to do but stare at myself in the mirror, wondering if I look like a supermodel and if that will help get me into college. Brooke Shields, Charlotte told us, went to Princeton. I also stare at the girl next to me in the mirror. Her blue dress matches her blue eyes. Her skin is like doll skin, not one pore. When they pull my hair back, I think my eyes might look nice.

In makeup the woman keeps drawing with a pencil inside my eye and I keep blinking and she keeps saying, It's easier if you relax. She has an assistant who stands next to us holding Q-tips but doesn't say anything. I am going to tell you this later too: There is a woman whose whole job was holding Q-tips. I try to make conversation, but neither of them is interested. I look for you in the mirror. You look up from your newspaper and wink at me from across the room. With one eye made up, my face looks lopsided. With both eyes painted, my face looks round.

At the next show, which we have to run across town to make on time, they are yelling because all of us girls are arriving late with glitter everywhere. Dozens of assistants are going around with sticky tape removing it from our faces and bodies.

When they finish my hair and makeup—another different kind of ponytail and beige foundation—they take me alone to practice walking down the runway in high heels.

Faster, says the casting director. Confident.

I find you backstage and you say, Look, it's Serena Williams.

Who's that?

The famous tennis player.

She's less than ten feet from us and surrounded by cameras. She looks like a celebrity. She has a tight dress and high heels and an entourage.

And over there, that's Mick Jagger.

Who?

You don't know him? The Rolling Stones!

I shrug.

Anyway, he's a very famous musician.

I didn't know you knew famous people, or cared. We almost never listen to the radio or watch TV. You and dad have thirty CDs total and we get six channels. You call women's magazines ridiculous.

When the actual show happens, about halfway down the runway I feel my arms swinging out of sync with my legs. I shuffle in a tight U-turn at the end of the runway, and again when I turn off to go backstage, unclear on how I am meant to change direction gracefully in heels. When we come out for the finale, while the audience claps, I can't keep up with the girl in front of me and a gap grows between us as I hold up all the girls in line behind me. When we leave I ask an agent who was in the audience how I looked, and he says, Beautiful, baby. I know he is lying and that I should be embarrassed to have asked.

On our way home, while we wait at airport security, you ask me what I'm feeling, what I think of all these people, all these adults.

So far modeling seemed both boring and degrading. They treated you as a soon-to-be-obsolete, inconvenient stage mom, never greeting you, pushing past you backstage. Nobody spoke to me, I suppose to make clear that I was only there to display my body in clothes for rich people. But it was a huge opportunity. I think of you and me and all the hours we put into As and internships and networking and how you snuck me into lectures at Harvard to hear Benazir Bhutto and Noam Chomsky speak. How ambition is a pact between us. How you made sure that when people came for dinner I knew how to sit with grown-ups and listen and also speak with confidence because everyone, including me, deserved respect. I give you the answer I think you want:

They all seem stupid and superficial, I say.

What? you whisper.

We are going through the metal detector.

When we finally walk away, you speak.

You are so disappointed in me. You cannot believe you raised me to think this way. Never, ever disrespect someone because of the work they do or because they care about different things.

We stay quiet the rest of the way home. When Dad picks us up and asks how it went, I let you tell the stories.

2.

You grew up during the Cold War, learning that the free market meant freedom and growth meant progress. You didn't live in the States, so it remained mythical. Instead you saw children starving abroad and felt bombs shake your house, but you survived, so there must have been something true about the saving grace of your Americanness.

You went to business school and started a car-sharing company. You told me the company was an example of the transformational power of capitalism, but that left off the ending of the story, that your company was taken away by investors who wanted more money and power.

Remember when you met them for the first time? I found you in the bathroom the night before, shaving your legs, your top lip covered in white chemical-smelling cream. I asked: What are you doing?

Using Nair* to get rid of my mustache.

And shaving your legs? You never shave.

You have to pick your battles.

The next day you met the first potential investor, wearing a suit you found at the thrift store in Central Square. It worked.

After that your start-up moves out of our house and into a big office building. Two cars become a fleet of forty. Customer service is no longer me on a scooter, sent out to help new members

---

* "Following the works of Michel Foucault, feminists have examined the mechanism through which women comply with disciplinary regimes of patriarchal power, noting especially the relationship between female bodies, surveillance, and the gaze (Bartky, 1998; Bordo, 1993; McNay, 1993). To Foucault, modern discipline operates not by coercion and direct force, but through self-surveillance and normalization. These modern technologies of power render bodies docile." Ashley Mears, "Discipline of the Catwalk: Gender, Power and Uncertainty in Fashion Modeling," *Ethnography* 9, no. 4 (2008): 431.

struggling to unlock doors. The company expands to Washington, D.C., and New York. And then it is time to raise money again.

Three consecutive one-hundred-degree days in September leave us inside the house with the shades pulled. You're having nightmares: A bloody corpse turns up in the trunk of one of the cars your start-up has leased, and nobody wants to deal with it, so you have to figure it out. You go to the garage and open the trunk and, yes, there it is, terrifying and beginning to smell. You realize you're late to pick up the kids. We're all little again. You close the trunk and hope the smell hasn't reached the inside of the car. You get into the driver's seat; the smell isn't obvious. You drive to the day care with the windows open and pick us up and take us home and park the car and wait for Dad to get home so you can go out again and deal with the body.

An investor calls you in the middle of the night. You need to leave right now and come to Central Park, he says. You jump up from bed and run out of the house and down the street in the pitch black. The sun is rising and you're still running, barefoot, in your underpants and sleep T-shirt. You are running through Central Park. Crowds of people are cheering for you. Yes! You are so committed. The T-shirt is getting shorter and shorter. Yes! You are doing it, you will do anything for this company. Yes! You realize only as they form a circle that you're there to be shot and killed. That is why they are cheering. That is what he has asked of you.

Then the lead investor pulls out two days before seven million dollars are supposed to land in the bank. That same month is the company's best: You celebrate its highest growth to date. You travel looking for investors. You prepare shutdown plans for the board.

You watch a falcon maul a pigeon outside your office window. When I get there after school, you show me all that's left: feathers and a stain on the concrete ledge.

Eventually you find the money—a women's investment group—but the newly expanded board takes the company anyway. You haven't slept in months. You are too tired to fight. The new CEO will do anything for money, you tell me. That's why the board picked him.

It was strange, you say, how physical the loss was. You tell me it felt like having no energy left. You couldn't even do laundry.

The new CEO was obviously picked for his maleness, because that is all he had on you. He takes triple the salary you took, and that was only counting the last six months, because before that you'd taken nothing, wanting so badly for the start-up to work.

I'm sixteen and we take more walks without the younger kids. I ask Dad and one of your brothers and Grandma and some of your close friends to write you letters to remind you that you are loved. I write one too and give them all to you with a book of photos from the cross-country bus trip we took. After I give you the album, you tell me that, since I could sense it, yes, you would kill yourself if it weren't for me and my brother and sister and Dad.

I won't, because that would probably ruin your lives, you say.

Yes, it would ruin our lives, I say.

Years later, when you read a draft of this book, you tell me we never had this conversation. You suggest it was something I must have imagined.

What is sacrificed to keep telling this coherent story of the American dream? I read once about how birds, maybe crows, changed their migratory path after one of them was shot and killed by a farmer. How thousands never stopped on that land again. How thousands agreed.

You calculate from the metrics Dad accidentally mentions when he comes home (he still works there) and from reports in the press how the company is doing. You figure out how many fewer cars there are on the streets, how much less emissions, how many more people have access to a car now who didn't before, what burden has been lifted. The only purposeful work, you tell me, is suffering reduced.

When I get up from my homework at night for a bathroom break, I stand in your doorway and mouth to Dad, Is she sleeping? He shakes his head.

3.

How much money would have to be on the tracks to make you jump in?

Danica, Molly, and I are waiting for the subway after school. It's the first week of senior year and it's still warm outside and we don't have homework yet.

Well, the biggest bill is a twenty, right? Or, like, can it be like a bundle of money? says Danica.

Any amount, but pretend you know how much, I say.

I'd jump in for a twenty anyway, if the train wasn't coming, she says. Better question: How much money would you have to be paid to have sex with someone?

Can you choose who the person is?

Of course not!

We all crack up.

I think a couple hundred, says Danica. She wrote a paper for history last year about why sex work should be legal.

What? No way, I say.

Then what? says Danica.

They both wait for my answer like I'm about to say I'm better than them. They are the only ones who know I was a model last week.

I don't know. I shrug.

After they get off, the train goes into the tunnel and I look at my reflection in the window. I think I have cheekbones and sexy lips. I think if I tilt my chin down, maybe I have "bedroom eyes," which is what you called them when we saw the first test photos.

Charlotte calls to tell you a client is ready to confirm Thursday in New York. Pay is $2,500 plus $2,500 usage, because they're running the ad the first Sunday in November in *The New York Times*. We agree immediately: A day of school could never be worth more than five thousand dollars.

You plan to call the school and tell them I'm sick Thursday morning. Why make a big deal out of this if we don't know what's really going to happen? you say. This could be the first and last time you make any money modeling.

You have to work, so I take the $20 Fung Wah bus to New York alone. The agency will charge $80 for me to stay in the model apartment for the night. Most of the ride I think about $5,000 minus $100 in expenses. Not enough to pay for college but, you say, at least I can use it to cover books and other school supplies. The only wage I know is minimum wage, $5.15. On the last page of my planner I do the math: $4,900 divided by $5.15 is 951 hours, or about twenty-four weeks working full time. Is this right? There are only fifty-two weeks in a year.

The shoot is in a bar. They keep moving me to the center or taking the other girls out of the shot. At the end of the day, they send all three of us to use a photo booth. After every flash the girls do a completely different pose: hands in hair, wink, blow kisses, go back-to-back, unbutton their shirts, pop their collars, stand up and bend over into the frame. It's like acting, except more humiliating, because they're being ditzy without a script.

When the strips develop, I look bad in every picture: bored, annoyed; even when I'm trying to laugh, my eyes look small and my cheeks look too big. The other girls look perfect. I am surprised they put me in front all day if this is how good the other girls look.

They send the girls back into the booth to shoot more, and the stylist takes me to try on sunglasses. Then all three of us do it again, me in sunglasses. I try to copy them without being obvious.

When I get home it's late, so you pick me up at the bus station. You ask how it went. Good! I say. Easy. Because what else am I supposed to say?

In less than a week Charlotte calls with another, even bigger job. They will pay me seven thousand dollars a day for a two-day shoot in Texas. Of course I miss school. You fly with me.

We've never been to Texas, but all we end up seeing is the highway, the studio, and the Applebee's where we eat dinner. We see stores that sell cowboy boots, and people really wearing them. I read that Bill Clinton wore cowboy boots when he campaigned, and I always imagined campaigning here, sitting at a picnic table in my own boots and jeans, drinking a beer, acting tough, being able to talk about time spent in the military and the economy. I ask you if I can buy a pair.

When will you ever wear them? They're really expensive, you say.

The art director tells you the brand has a store in Boston.

Really, you say. I never knew that. How many customers does it take to support a store?

Fifteen to twenty-five, he says.

When I get up from hair and makeup for a bathroom break and I walk by you, you whisper, How's it going? I say, Boring, and you whisper, Yeah, but can you fathom an easier job? Just count your money.

On the way home you want to talk about modeling. You tell me: I don't think you should tell anyone how much money you are making.

You don't?

Imagine your friends comparing their wages to what you just made. It will make them feel bad. Think how unfair it is for you to say, I made seven thousand dollars in one day. Anyone who works hard for their money will feel kind of degraded.

you're a gemini

1.

She called her observations:
Notes on the Male Mind.   (Frances Perkins)[1]

Noted:
how to make herself agreeable
to everyone.   (Cleopatra)[2]

Begin:
to dress and comport in a way that
remind[s] men of their mothers.   (Frances Perkins)[3]

Cultivate:
a natural style.   (Marilyn Monroe)[4]

Wear:
a beaded, scalloped necklace
on the days you cannot
express dissent verbally.   (Ruth Bader Ginsburg)[5]

Ask yourself:
Do you look like someone who
is credible?   (Anita Hill)[6]

2.

You come with me to LA because you still think sixteen is too young to be going on all these shoots alone.

On set I bend down to fix my shoe, and when I look up you're gone. When I come back to the motor home with the stylist and his assistant to change outfits, I find you sitting alone. You whisper: The photographer sent one of his assistants to tell me to wait in here because it would make you more comfortable. Are you uncomfortable with me on set?

My heart hurts and my stomach hurts and I cannot bear you thinking that might be true, especially because you came all the way here to be with me.

No, I whisper, I want you with me.

I guess it makes them uncomfortable, you say, tilting your head toward the crew smoking outside. They can't treat you like a sex object when your mom is on set.

When we get back home, Dad has taken the kids to visit our grandparents so you and I fall asleep together in your bed to an episode of *Wife Swap*. In the morning I wake up alone and come down to the kitchen to find you. I'm wearing what I slept in: my new flesh-tone tank top from H&M, no bra, underwear. It's hot. You look at me and say: I know I shouldn't say this, but you're going to make some man very happy one day.

What? Who says that?

I know, I know.

I guess it's a compliment. You are tired. You rest your chin on my shoulder, and I hold you.

A big story confirms. This is what we've been waiting for, says Charlotte, adding that it would be better for you not to come. The photographer, Alex, works on a closed set.

Alex is important. Bringing your mom would look immature, and I know you can handle it, says Charlotte. Anyway, you don't have to worry, she says. He has kids, he gets it.

When he arrives on set, I'm already in hair and changed into a robe, and he comes up behind me and just looks at me in the mirror. He doesn't say anything. Instead, he touches my hair, pulls a piece from behind my ear, and smooths it along my temple with his thumb. Maybe mess the hair up a little? he says to the hairdresser. Nerves connect my hair and my cheek to my spine to my vagina. He tilts his head at my reflection and rests the weight of his hands on my shoulders. She's amazing, he says to the room, then massages my shoulders. He winks in the mirror and finally speaks to me. Nice to meet you. Then he steps away so the hairdresser can keep working.

When he's not staring at me, I stare at him. Our eyes meet in the mirror a couple times and I look down quickly. When I check, he is still staring. Finally on set, I look into his camera and know he's looking back.

When we start shooting, he asks everyone to leave, and then he speaks quietly, only to me. He says: Fuck, you're sexy, fuck, you're beautiful.

Even though he probably says it to everyone, nobody has ever told me I'm sexy. Nobody has ever touched me like that. Is this how adults speak?

Close your eyes, he tells me.

I do.

Raise your chin, lean your head back.

I know I'm supposed to be thinking about sex. But I have no reference points. I can't even think of a movie sex scene.

He shoots for a long time until the stylist comes over and tells him: You have it.

Okay, he says, clicking one more time and then letting the camera hang by his side. Fuck, I can't stop, he says, and now he is looking right into my eyes when he speaks.

We take a break because Benjamin, the art director from the magazine, comes and wants to look at the pictures. I get back into a robe and sit on a couch and wait. My back is to them, but I hear them going through the images on the computer. Fuck, fuck, fuck, dude, they say.

When we start shooting again, I start to think Alex is taking the picture when I breathe out, so I start letting my breath out and not breathing for a few shots. And then I notice maybe he likes it when I breathe in too, like he's clicking with my breath. So I breathe in and out with the shots through my lips, seeing if I can make the breath do whatever it is he likes by exaggerating the expansion of my chest with each inhale and hollowing it out with each exhale. My heart is pounding and I can't tell if it's because I'm cold, or nervous, if it's the way I'm breathing, or if it's Alex.

Becoming a supermodel might be all about power. Letting the photographer feel he controls you, that when he tells you to close your eyes, lift your chin, open your lips, that you do it for him. You breathe for him. And when you open your eyes and look into the camera, it's to look at him. He brings you pleasure. Or maybe that's just what Alex likes.

Even when he isn't shooting, I listen when he speaks and watch where he moves. My eyes follow him. I think he feels my attention, my body communicating with his. He doesn't speak to me directly, so there is no opportunity for any other type of conversation anyway.

3.

Back home I dream I'm in your house, Alex. I don't go inside your kids' bedrooms, I just peek before pulling the doors back closed: This is the little one's room, neat, with a converted crib; this is the older one's, with a twin bed and books. I sleep in your bed. I shower in your shower. I cook in your kitchen. Then I clean everything. Hair out of the drain, off the sink; I find a single long strand left in your bed. Take the trash out. Replace the bag just so. I am afraid you will know I have been here. No, not you. You know; you left me the keys. Your wife. I don't want her to know. But I have been. I know the morning light in your room, the length of the hall, the neat stack of art books on the windowsill in your bathroom.

How can I shoot with you again?

I don't know it yet, but in a few months you will stop shooting me and I'll only ever see you again when I'm on the runway and you're sitting in the front row and I'm looking straight forward for the cameras but catch your face in my peripheral vision. And then twice more, from across the room at industry parties.

At first I wrote to you, Mom. Then you became Alex. And you taught me the first requirement of being a model is to try to fake intimacy. Otherwise one day I give my whole self over, and the next it's like we're strangers.

Most of the time this is for you—the customer, the audience. You are imagined, of course, but I have been imagining you since the beginning.

Models perform intimacy. We perform for you and your attention; your gaze turns a performance into a real thing. When you look, we enter a relationship. That is why it made sense to tell the story of modeling to you.

4.

I find a book on the top shelf called *Women's Health* and take it to my room. The book has one chapter about sex. Two pages on how you can orgasm from sex or from just touching yourself.

The book says to touch all different parts and then focus on the clitoris. It says to touch your breasts. It has diagrams with arrows and dotted lines. After the house is asleep, I take the book out from under my covers, review the diagrams, and turn off the lights to try it. It says a big part is mental, so I try to think about what sex is. I put my finger inside my vagina to see if that feels like sex. It doesn't feel like anything. Maybe I'm one of the women who can't orgasm; it says 30 percent of women don't orgasm but still enjoy sex. I think about you, Alex, and what would happen if we had gone alone to your hotel room, as you suggested the second time we shot together. You asked if I wanted to come up to see the pictures from our first shoot before they were published. I paused, trying to figure out what you wanted, and while I was thinking, you said, No, never mind, we should get going. I think about you, and the song you kept playing on set. *Remember when I moved in you? And from your lips* . . . It doesn't work.

At school a teacher, Mr. C, asks me if I have any crushes, and I tell him no. We have to pick an adviser this year to check in with about college planning. I was going to ask a history teacher I loved, but now, with all the school days I'm missing, I need someone who won't bother me about absences as long as my grades are good. I ask him. Of course, Mr. C grins, Bring me the form to sign.

I do have crushes: writers. Updike, Bukowski, Nabokov, Coetzee.

I hate putting them together like that, they don't deserve it.

Then again, they can't see me. They don't know I've taken them home to meet my parents. They don't care that I read them in bed.

The next time we shoot, you ask if I'll shoot nudes, the artistic kind, and I laugh. I let myself enjoy your grin, mischievous, inviting me into something adult and intimate. I am not clear on what you want or think of me, if my laugh annoys you, or if you think of me at all, because you still barely speak to me. I'm only sixteen, I say. But you won't be forever, you say.

Maybe you prefer me when I don't talk, maybe I am more enchanting without words. Does my voice sound like Updike's girl-queen in the A&P? "Her voice kind of startled me, the way voices do when you see the people first, coming out so flat and dumb yet kind of tony, too."[7]

In the afternoon your wife visits the set. She doesn't speak to me either. I ask the hairdresser if she comes in often. And he says to me, You know why she's here, and raises his eyebrows.

Neither of you know me and I don't know you. Or maybe you know something about me that even I don't know.

When I leave the job, I call Mom. How was it? she asks. Were you your charismatic, confident self?

I don't know, I say. If I were really charismatic, they'd want to talk to me.

Maybe everything Mom believes about me isn't true.

I am trying, like Mom said, to be respectful and understand the perspective of these photographers, these fashion people. Even when they do vulgar things, like when a photographer takes a lip gloss and smears it around his mouth and mimes oral sex. I'm not sure if that's just for show or if he really wants to have sex. When I talk back and call him a pervert, it's just for show.

Until now I had found that powerful men love little girls who want to be powerful men. They love hearing my mile time and sharing that theirs is something to aspire to. They love calling themselves my mentor. Like when Mom introduced me to one of her board members, a former cabinet secretary to a governor. He invites me to do homework at his office around the corner from my school. I consider it. He would be a powerful friend to have. But Mom tells me, I don't think you need to take him up on it, it's a weird offer.

I think powerful men like that I have learned their words: VC, angel investor, series A, series B, minimum viable product, equity, term sheet. I think they like that I can talk politics, that I push back, but only so much, because then I nod while they explain.

But now? I am powerless because I do not know what men are thinking, which is how I end up reading all of Bukowski in about a month.

"hey, what you doing?"
"doin? I'm going to fuck you!" I put my finger into her cunt and moved it back and forth. "I'm going to fuck you!"[8]

Writers are explicit and confessional. They have sex with women. I don't see myself in the women, but then, I'm not reading books to learn about women.

You confirm me for another job. Charlotte says you're obsessed. We're on location and we all go out to dinner together. We are walking up the steps into this little restaurant when someone makes a joke about me being jailbait. They are all laughing. Jail-what? I ask. Nobody answers me. Jail-what did they say? I ask the makeup artist.

Ignore them, he says.

I just didn't hear it.

They said you're jailbait. But they mean it as a compliment.

Okay, I say. I have no idea what the word means.

We all sit in a booth and I look at the menu because I don't really know how to hang with you. I slide the heart charm on my necklace back and forth and look for something to eat.

Who gave you the necklace? you ask. You still rarely speak to me, and my breath catches.

I know I'm probably supposed to say a boyfriend or something, but I can't come up with a lie in time.

My mom. It was hers when she was a teenager.

Oh my god, who are you? They are all laughing.

Suddenly I'm very sad. I don't know why, but I feel like I want to protect Mom from this, protect us. Our relationship is not a joke, something for them to enjoy the way they enjoy my new breasts and my blushes. I keep looking at the menu and they start talking about someone I don't know, and a house someone just bought. I laugh when they laugh.

I ask Mom what jailbait is when I get home, and she says it's a disgusting concept, that an underage girl is baiting older men into sex, which would be illegal. Where did you hear that? Set, I say with a shrug. Gross, she says.

The idea that sleeping with one of these men would land them in jail seems very dramatic. Having sex would be absurd. But illegal?

I tell Mom that a man is following me on the subway to school and that he photographed me with a disposable camera, and she tells me to report him to the police. He's not the only man who has followed me, but he sticks out. He has thinning orange hair, slit nostrils, freckles, and near-translucent skin; he is tall and skinny; he is an easy target. I tell her he looks like Voldemort. The cops find him right away.

We have to go to the courthouse and sit in a room across from him while the judge says to us both: I will issue a one-hundred-yard restraining order. This means he cannot be in the station with you. If you come into the station when he is there, he will need to leave. If you are on the same subway car, he will need to leave.

She dismisses us and the man stays behind with the two cops and the judge. I cannot remember if we learn his name. Or if he ever looked up. Whatever record this created for this lonely forty-something-year-old, I knew it would have been easier for me to bear his advances. It would always be this way. I could experience without feeling; I was much tougher than sad, silly men. I start biking to school.

On set it's the same. My superpower is I don't allow myself to feel except for what I'm sure I'm supposed to be feeling. For example: I allow myself to think about why I might feel excited, giddy, why my nerves tingle, and I try to feel this more. I also don't allow myself to speak unless they ask me a question, because every time I do, it gets me in trouble. A call from a casting agent to my agent to complain that I think I'm better than everyone else, talking about school and doing homework backstage. From a client to my agent, saying I'm childish and shouldn't tell people I bought my new shoes from the children's section. An assistant telling me to hush, we're at work and now is not the time for chatting or laughing.

A $30K day confirms. With you again. You tell me to throw my head back, close my eyes, and open my legs. I say I don't want to. You tell everyone to clear the set and ask me what's wrong. It will look too sexual, I say, staring at the floor.

Mom told me don't close my eyes or arch my back and don't open my legs. My face is hot. My body is hot. My armpits are damp. I keep my arms clamped down because you are leaning in so close to me.

I promise I won't make it look that way, you say. I'll take one so you can see. You take a shot of me doing the pose.

The hairdresser comes in and you tell him to give-us-a-sec. You show me the picture on the back of the camera.

I can't tell. I wish Mom were here to decide.

I look beautiful in the picture. My waist is tiny, my butt is round, my profile backlit looks like a perfect Barbie-doll profile. I guess it's fine. I look good. It doesn't look like porn. I don't know. You wipe a tear off my face with your thumb and raise my chin with your fingers. I'm mortified and look away and try to breathe slowly. I am glad for the comfort of a warm hand, and for almost being held by you.

I wonder if I don't have good intuition. When I am uncomfortable, I remind myself it is because I'm too young to know better. When I can leave the set to ask by phone or text, Mom and Charlotte tell me what's okay. I am being given the chance of a lifetime. I have to be professional. This is what the job is, and I am too tough to be embarrassed and too brave to be intimidated. Soon nothing will bother me. The way to stop reacting is to put the self away so there's nobody to offend, to humiliate, to blame, to ignore.

I tell myself to be humble and respectful, which means listen to everyone else, I'm not important yet. I get out of the way. I don't cry, don't laugh, don't smile unless they smile. I say, Thank you. I say, Sorry.

Charlotte emails the scans of the very first shoot we did together the day they are published. I'm at school, but I read her text telling me she's sent them and a nervous thrill grips me. How intense it is to be in front of your camera, and now there are photos of it I can see, everyone can see. I skip announcements to run to the computer lab, but it's full. I go to Mr. C's office and ask him if I can use his computer. He gives me his chair and stands behind me.

The files download slowly, revealing my forehead, then startling hungry eyes, open mouth, my chest, then the outline of my nipples entirely visible. Oh my god, the photos are sexy. I didn't know I could express anything so sexual.

Mr. C can't stop staring at the computer even when I glance back at him. You look . . . He stares. Wow, Cam. You look . . .

I log out. His eyes are glued to me.

Thanks, I say, slinging my backpack on, pleased he's at a loss for words. The contradiction of me in my Payless skater shoes, boy's pants, and hand-knitted sweater and those images where I'm recognizable, wearing barely any makeup, but something completely other. How much freedom I feel, being something he cannot have or grade or determine, something he, an adult, a teacher, cannot even beat me at.

I walk to class and start to feel upset with myself. How did I not know my nipples were going to be so visible? I will have to show Mom to see if they went too far.

They're sexier than I thought they'd be, Mom says.

How could I have known? I say.

I think they would be embarrassing to have on the cover of *Time* magazine if I ran for president, and I'm glad Mom doesn't bring it up. Thinking about it makes me angry. I haven't done anything wrong.

5.

By winter I've been modeling for three months and we have decided it's fine for me to work alone, so I go to Paris without Mom.
After the first shoot day is over, Charlotte calls and says the magazine called her and said it isn't going well. She tells me I need to
learn how to model. She says, You're not a new girl anymore. I
don't cry. I stare out the window at Paris in the dark. It's all mo-
torcycles and cars and rain.

I manage to say in a level voice that I thought it went okay.

How am I messing it up? Is there anything easier than modeling? I stay quiet.

Charlotte is still talking: Tomorrow you need to participate.
Do whatever they ask. Look at their references. You have to look
at magazines, see how the pros do it. If you want to keep modeling, you need to learn how to move, figure out which ways your
face looks good, pay attention to the light, okay?

Do I want to keep modeling? Obviously I shouldn't walk away
from the money. I wish Mom were here. I wish I weren't alone.
In the hotel room I want to call, but international rates are expensive. And what would I say? I'm not doing a good job posing?
Standing in front of a camera? I turn on the shower. At least I'm
not alone when the warm water is running over me.

The hotel phone rings in the bathroom. It's the hairdresser.
Come downstairs and have dinner with us. We're in the restaurant.

Okay, I say. Why are they inviting me if they don't like me? If
I go, will they like me?

I put back on my miniskirt and sweater. In the elevator, my
legs start itching. I use the corner of my key card to scratch
through my tights without starting a run.

The hairdresser looks like a guy who could be in the Hells Angels. He's wearing motorcycle boots and is probably 6' 3" and three hundred pounds. Finn, the photographer, is wearing a leather jacket and a ripped shirt and paint-splattered boots. Sitting on red-and-gold velvet chairs in the hotel restaurant at a tiny circular marble table, they look like they're visiting from a different movie set. They both stand up to hug and double kiss me, even though we just saw each other at the studio an hour ago. They smell like alcohol and cigarettes.

Want some red? Finn asks, holding up a bottle.

No, thanks.

How old are you again?

They both already asked. They just want to hear me say it.

Sixteen.

You're legal drinking age here, girly, the hairdresser says, patting my leg.

You're gonna get us in trouble, says Finn.

I laugh.

I don't know what else to say, so I stop talking. They talk and I don't know how to talk about what they are talking about. Someone got fired. She's fucking who? They don't ask me anything else, so I just laugh when they laugh and eat my food.

When I'm done I can barely keep my eyes open.

I really should sleep, I tell them. I'm jet-lagged.

Oh, you're young. Stay for a drink, or at least for a dessert?

My elbows are on the table. I lean my head on my hands and look up at them. I feel tired and sloppy.

God, we have to shoot a Lolita story on you! says Finn.

I want to say, But I thought you didn't like working with me. Instead I say: "Lolita, or the Confession of a White Widowed Male."[9]

Why did I say that? I'm such a jerk. Do they think I'm talking about them? So I add: It's the first line. Did I want that badly for them to know I had read the book? I just memorized the first sentence because of this tradition Mom and Grandpa and I have of memorizing and sharing good first lines with each other. My favorite is from *Charlotte's Web:* " 'Where's Pa going with that ax?' said Fern to her mother as they set the table for breakfast."[10]

All right, nerd, says Finn. We're gonna go to a bar.

The itching starts again when I lie down. I can't sleep. I'm not tired anymore. I'm scratching my legs so hard I think even if the skin came off the itching wouldn't stop. There are bumps all over my leg. I turn the lights on. My legs are red and covered in scrapes and some blood. I go to the bathroom and try putting on the hotel lotion, but it stings and I itch more.

I turn the lights off. Is this from shaving? I lie flat on my back and put my hands under my butt. Leave it alone, leave it alone. I gave myself the night off homework, so I should fall asleep, rest.

In the morning my legs look fine. Maybe if the rash had spread and I had an allergic reaction to something, I could have gotten on a plane back home. Probably not. They'd probably cover it with makeup. I want to be anywhere but on this set where everyone thinks I'm a terrible model.

I look at magazines during hair. One editorial is of a girl in the back of a car. I can't really replicate any of her poses in a studio. She's leaning her head on the wheel, then she's got her legs up on the dashboard, then hanging out the window. The only studio shoot I find is of a girl jumping. Wouldn't it be awkward to just start jumping? Maybe that's what I'm supposed to do.

Finn clicks and I put my hands on my hips, stare into the camera lens, let my lips open a little. I take one hand down and let it hang. I look in profile. I cross my arms. I cross my legs.

Open your legs, he says.

I open my legs wide. Try to commit and not worry about looking silly.

Not that wide, says Finn.

I shuffle my feet back together. I feel unsteady in heels. I don't know what they want. The stylist, chain-smoking and mumbling in French, comes in and adjusts all the clothes, pinching the cigarette in the corner of his mouth, exhaling from the other side into my face.

He says, Can you give us a little more energy? He says it loud enough that the whole room can hear.

Like jumping?

We can try that, says Finn. On my count. One, two, three! One, two, three. Maybe less, try just a little hop. One, two, three! One, two, three! Just a step now.

Can I take the heels off?

No, keep them on, says the stylist. He looks at the back of Finn's camera. They look back at me.

Let's try a few more walking, says Finn. Smaller movements, okay?

Okay. I move to the right of my mark.

When you're ready, says Finn, looking through his camera.

I walk across the set. Shoulders back. Not swinging the arms too much. I feel like crying. I don't know what they want. But I am in this studio in Paris and I have to shoot this story and be here all day.

Let's clear the set, Finn says.

The stylist hustles everyone away, comes back to adjust my clothes, then hides behind a V-flat.

Finn comes up to me. I'm standing still on my mark. He puts his hands on my shoulders. It's just us.

Just loosen up a bit, okay? He squeezes my shoulders. Okay?

I force myself to speak. Okay, I whisper without looking at him.

Let's just try a couple things without everyone watching. He releases my shoulders and asks his assistant to bring a stool and a modeling stand to set. I sit on the stool. I put my arms on the black felt stand. He places my hands on my face, places my pinky and ring fingers between my lips, brushes some hair from my forehead.

He says: Make it feel natural.

I'm worried it looks too sexual to have my fingers in my mouth. But I am glad to feel my hand on my face. I'm not alone. I am here with me. And I don't think I can tell him I won't do it. He's trying to help me.

Breathe, he says.

I exhale.

Look at me.

I look into the camera.

You're so sexy, he says.

I try to hear him and feel strong. He likes me, I think. He thinks I'm sexy. I can do this. I think about last night, how he wanted me at dinner, wanted me to drink and stay out with them, how he looked at me when I said I was sixteen.

Turn in profile. Chin up. Make your neck longer.

I think about shooting with Alex and how to infatuate someone without words.

Maybe it's just the stylist who dislikes me. To make him happy is a whole other task. He doesn't want me, he wants my allegiance. He comes on set and tells me to shout. I shout. More real, he says. Howl like a dog. I do it. He says, Louder.

If the stylist wants me to look ugly, my back humped, my face contorted, if he wants me to be a witch, if he wants me to be a child, if he wants me to be a clown, if he wants me to be tied, like I am now, into a corset with my breasts swelling like water balloons, if he wants my eyes closed, if he wants me to laugh, then that's what I'm supposed to do. As soon as we've got the shot he walks off set and back to the changing area. I try to chat with him. I ask where he is from. He pretends not to hear me and speaks in French to his assistant.

At the end of the day Finn puts all the photos up together on the monitor and flips through them. I think: It's not about getting a shot right, because the ones from yesterday look good. It's about being the right girl. The girl they want. It's about letting them be in charge, letting them think they made you.

6.

Dad says the phone is for me, it's Jack. I have no idea who Jack is. I run upstairs and pick up the phone in my parents' bedroom, I got it, Dad, I say, and he hangs up. I hear the British accent and figure out it's Jack, the important stylist, calling our home number.

Hi, darling. Your agent gave me your number. I hope this is a good time?

For sure. What's up?

Alex said you could tell me about the game you play with these colorful jelly bracelets? We're shooting them today.

In middle school I overheard two girls talking about the snap game on the bus. I didn't think it was interesting then, or even true, but I told a makeup artist about it one day because she was wearing a big pile of these bracelets and I was grasping for conversation. Then she made me tell the photographer. Then everyone was obsessed with the story and they kept making me tell it again. That's how I figured out it was a story people in fashion liked to hear, so I started telling it more on other sets. I even have a couple jelly bracelets, two black, one clear blue with sparkles, conversation starters.

I didn't play, I just heard about it at my middle school, I tell Jack. The rules are just, like, if a guy can pop a bracelet off a girl's wrist, she has to do whatever that color means. Like kissing, blow job, sex, whatever.

And the colors mean different things? he asks. I just wanna know for reference.

Yeah, I mean, I don't know them all, except that white is snowballing.

What's snowballing?

It's when a guy comes in a girl's mouth and then she puts it in another girl's mouth and so on down a line of girls until the last girl swallows.

Jack laughs. And the other colors?

I'm not sure. One is, like, kissing with tongue, sex, blow job, stuff like that.

Okay, he laughs. Thank you, Cameron. See you soon.

I text Charlotte to tell her Jack called.

"How'd it go?" she texts back.

"Good. He said, 'See you soon,' so maybe he'll book me again."

I go back downstairs, grateful nobody was listening. It's a lazy Sunday: My younger sister is building a maze for her cat out of old boxes. I join my brother reading comics on the floor. Mom and Dad read the rest of the paper on the couch.

Nobody at work cares much about what I have to say, so when they do, I tell the same story a dozen times: I have a friend whose roommate decided to try waxing the hair off her nipples. Using my palm like the paper that takes off wax, I rip my hand away from my breast. I look down. She sees one hair left and decides to tweeze it. She pulls—I pretend to pull a hair from my nipple—and the hair just keeps coming out. I hold the pretend tweezers half a foot from my breast and look, with surprise, at the invisible long hair. So she gets scissors and cuts the hair and then—pause—she faints onto the floor. My friend hears the crash and brings her to the ER and they tell her she's cut a nerve. Nerves apparently look like hairs. I cross my arms over my breasts and shiver.

People grab their own chests. Their bodies feel something. But also they've been watching me grab my own tits. They're turned on, horrified, excited. They don't forget me. They ask me to tell the story again to someone else. And there's a new crew to entertain every week. This is part of being a model. But a script is also a type of speechlessness.

Mom is listening when Charlotte calls to go over options. I'm on hold for a big campaign. She wants me to come down to New York to shoot a portrait for an important magazine.

I'll have to miss school, I say. Do you really think it's worth it for just one picture?

It's really important. This is the first time they're ready to confirm you.

Okay, let me think about it.

Don't think too long. Also, that catalog client wants you again.

For how many days?

So far just one.

Are they paying travel days?

I don't know, let me ask.

Can they confirm two days at least? Because I'd have to miss school for it too.

When I get off the phone, Mom says, Listening to you negotiate is impressive. You really have it down to an art. You know how to hold your own.

You think?

Yes, she says, wow.

In the spring when we get a week off from school, we are supposed to find an internship in something that interests us and then write about it. In the past I worked on local political campaigns. But this year Mom suggests I just work. I tell her one of the rules is that you can't make money. She says the school doesn't understand. They don't know how much you're getting paid and would never tell their own daughters not to take the money. I am on option for a big campaign that week that is going to shoot in Paris. Mom tells me to lie and say I'm shooting editorial, and editorial doesn't pay. They can't expect you to give away this money because of some dopey school policy, she says. It's a once-in-a-lifetime opportunity. So I lie. Charlotte lies all the time too. She tells me to lie to clients about what I'm doing. I'm telling them you have an exam, she says when we choose one job over another.

By summer vacation, my plan is to go to New York and work as much as I can.

When I get to the models' apartment the girls are still up. The couches in the living room have sheets thrown over them to catch crumbs and makeup smears. Amina is on one texting. Louise and Rona sit on the other watching TV.

The house chaperone, Devyn, makes a big deal when I walk in. Oh my god, she shouts, you're killing it! Charlotte showed me your editorial. Girl! You're so hot. She hugs me.

The girls doing laundry and snacking in the kitchen disperse. In the living room they turn up the volume and lie on the floor. Only Fernanda sticks around. She's making a stir-fry, pouring fish and vegetables into a pan from a freezer bag. Oil spits on the stove.

Devyn waves a magazine. We're reading horoscopes! What are you?

I forget, I say. My birthday is June 14.

Ohhhkay. She scans the page. You're a Gemini. Oh my god, this is so perfect!

She walks to the living room so the other girls can hear. I'm still in my backpack and coat, on the perimeter.

Gemini. You're a goddess, a sex icon, a Marilyn. She cackles. Don't deny it, babe! I think it's your calling!

Louise flicks her eyes from the TV to glare at me. She's an ex-evangelical from Florida who talks about sex and doesn't put concealer over her pimples, even for castings, and always has a quick insult for whoever dares speak to her. But she's also one of the few Americans (and fluent English speakers) and always says hi, even if it's "Hi, bitch."

I dunno about that stuff, I say to Dev, trying to ignore Louise. I look for my phone charger in my backpack. It could all apply to anyone.

No, babe, I saw you in that red dress. You're iconic.

You know me, I'm nerdy. Anyway, I gotta go to bed, I'm tired.

You can't fool us, missy, she laughs.

Goodnight, goddess, yells Louise as I walk down the hall.

I shower off the hair and makeup from work and realize Devyn was right: I have to be an icon if I'm going to succeed.

Amina must have the day off, because she's still passed out when I get up, her headphones in, her blankets falling onto the floor. I tuck them behind the ladder when I come down from the top bunk, and change quickly into tights and my black-and-white casting dress.

In the kitchen Louise and Rona are making oatmeal in the microwave. Rona is also American and best friends with Louise.

Good morning, I say. Rona smiles. Louise doesn't say anything. Any good cereal left? I ask.

Charlotte canceled the Lucky Charms from the delivery, says Rona.

What? Why?

She wants us to eat healthy and not be fat.

We're not fat, that's crazy.

Well, model-fat, obviously.

I'm gonna tell her to put it back.

And she will, says Louise, because everything's about you. Or didn't you notice?

Um, okay.

The rest of us can't eat Lucky Charms, so don't bother, unless you only care about yourself.

Okay, I'm sorry—

I'm sorry, I'm sorry, Louise whines.

Rona shrugs and follows Louise with their oatmeal to the living room. I pour Grape-Nuts and join them.

Do you have castings today? I ask.

Every day, says Louise.

Me too, I say. Wanna go together?

We have to go to the agency first, says Rona.

Oh, me too, actually. (I don't, I'm just desperate for company.)

They leave later than I should, but I'm glad not to be alone. On the train I ask if Charlotte is their booker too.

She's head of new faces, says Rona, so I guess sort of. But I don't really like her. I try to talk to the other agents mostly.

You don't like her? Why not?

Well, she'll, like, call and tell me not to go out if she hears we're planning to, and then she'll be like, Whatever you do, don't drink. Alcohol makes you fat and makes your face fat. She measured my hips in front of the whole office the other day. It was fucked up. She pinched my fat and said super loud: These hips need to match your card.

Then change my card, bitch, Louise interjects. They laugh.

Why are you even staying at the shitty models' apartment? Louise asks me. Don't you have enough money to, like, get a hotel? She stares at me, waiting for an answer.

It's not like I'm here with a client, I say. Nobody's paying for me to be here.

Whatever, she says. She puts her headphones in.

What else does Charlotte do? I ask Rona.

I mean, listen, it's not like she's the worst. It's her job, after all. It's just, like, I think she could be nicer about shit. I'm here and I left high school to try to make this happen.

You left high school? I say.

Just two years early, I'm gonna get my GED. But it's not like I had a choice. They wouldn't have signed me if I didn't. Now if I don't earn enough, they aren't gonna keep me anyway. But I think I will.

We part ways at the agency and I spend the day going from casting to casting by myself. They are endless and boring. They tell us to walk or try something on, they Polaroid our faces front-on and in profile, if we're lucky they may stick our cards or Polaroids onto a big wall with pictures of all the girls who are being considered. Sometimes when we arrive they ask, How are you? or Where are you from? or How old are you? But it is hard to say anything interesting in response. I tell them my birthday is this week. I tell them I'm good, but a little sore from helping my dad sand floors. I try to find something interesting to share. But they usually look at their phones or interrupt to tell me to do the next thing, stand there, try this, get measurements done. An assistant with a tape measure wraps our waists and hips and calls out numbers to compare with our comp cards, which are amended by pen, any differences noted with annoyance, and loudly. I realize that they don't want us to talk; it takes up time and bores them. But what else can I do to affect the outcome? When the casting is over, nobody talks or looks at us, which is how we know we're finished. Or sometimes, if I we stand there too long, an assistant comes over and thanks us quietly or just says, You can go. My only relief is calling Mom or Charlotte between appointments. I dissect each one trying to figure out how to do better. When Charlotte can't answer, she texts to ask how it's going.

At my last casting I bump into Gabi and Fernanda, who are also staying at the model apartment. We go home together and Fernanda tells us about her ex. It's hard, she says, when you travel all the time and they are back home spending your money. My mom told me to leave him. But we talked every night and I'm here alone, so it took me too long, you know? We nod. Gabi is even younger than me. She uses pads instead of tampons because she is a virgin. I'm happy not to have to lie when Fernanda asks if we've had boyfriends. We both shake our heads no. That's so cute. You're too cute.

After dinner some of the girls start doing hair and makeup on the floor of the living room, plugging in hair irons next to the TV on mute. One of the agents, Chris, is taking us out tonight to some event. Fernanda is playing R. Kelly's "Ignition" from her phone. When he sings, "Bounce bounce," some of the girls bounce and actually look like they are in a music video. They shake their hair, lift their chins, freshly glossed lips catch the television's blue light, and they smile with their eyes closed. Then they all crack up.

We all take turns using the bathrooms, where the light is better. When it's my turn Fernanda starts the song over. I hear them all sing, "Got every man in here wishin'."

The only thing I can think of to wear is a shirtdress I got when I was working in London. I pull it on and look in the bathroom mirror. It's long-sleeved and baggy, but at least it's as short as the outfits they are wearing.

Chris is already waiting downstairs in a limo for us. I think I'm the luckiest man alive, he says when we all pile in. Everyone laughs.

The party is at a big restaurant on West Broadway. When we get there Fernanda whispers to me, Free drinks, before following the girls to the bar and leaving me with the agent I barely know.

Chris is saying hi to people and I'm just following him around. Because what else am I supposed to do? Fernanda brings him a drink. God you're perfect, he tells her. She clinks his glass.

Cameron, says Chris, pulling me into a conversation, I wanted you to meet someone. A man stands up from his table to double kiss me.

Nice to meet you, I say over the music. Chris turns his back and starts talking to someone else.

The man leans in and says, so close to my ear his breath goes down my ear canal, Are you enjoying New York?

I lean toward his ear, but not that close. Yes, it's fun.

I lean back, pretending to bob my head to the music to get a better look at him. He's maybe sixty, wearing a suit, and he doesn't look like he works in fashion. I lean in and ask, Do you work in fashion?

No, but I'd love to take you shopping tomorrow.

Now I'm confused. Um, that's okay, I say.

Anywhere you want, Bloomingdale's, Bergdorf. I look for Chris or any of the girls, but it's dark and I don't see anyone. Then I find Fernanda dancing near the bar.

I see my friend, I say. Then louder, Nice to meet you, and walk quickly away.

Fernanda grabs my hands when I walk up. Cam-eh-rhone, she sings, and lifts my arms. What are you drinking?

What are you having?

Vodka cranberry. It's so good.

Okay, I'll have that.

She leans into the bar and orders for me. She hands me the drink and we cheers. It tastes metallic. She goes back to dancing with the other girls. I take a few sips out of the tiny straw and look around.

When the song they like is over, I ask Fernanda if she thinks I'll be able to get a cab home from here. Of course, she says, but I'll walk you out. She hails one for me and gives me a hug. See you in the morning, love.

As soon as the taxi pulls away I realize I probably don't have enough money. I count my bills.

Sorry, I say, I only have six dollars. Can you just let me out when the meter hits five?

I know the way back from Broadway.

My phone wakes me up at seven. It's my seventeenth birthday and I'm working. Two days of catalog. Who wouldn't want to make day rates on their birthday? At the end of the second day they get me a carrot cake and sing me "Happy Birthday." Charlotte calls and asks if I was surprised. She asks did I notice it had no raisins, just the way I like it. Oh my god, you told them that too? You're so incredible, I say.

The client has paid for a plane ticket home, and Dad picks me up when I land. Mom is still up. I tell them about going out with Chris.

To a fashion party at a bar? Mom asks.

What did you order to drink? says Dad, amused.

What the other girls ordered, cranberry vodka.

Did you drink it? Mom asks.

I had some but mostly just held it in my hand and then put it back on the bar.

Mom and Dad are cracking up.

Who do these people think you are?

We all laugh.

how to make herself agreeable

1.

To photograph is to appropriate the thing photographed. It means putting oneself into a certain relation to the world that feels like knowledge—and, therefore, like power.

—SUSAN SONTAG, *On Photography*

This is what the camera teaches you: a quick way to enamor, or simply to please, is to give up claims to authorship.

Claim: If you let the person looking through the lens feel that they are not a witness but a creator, that your body is only responding to their direction / to their desires, you let them become the author.

Proof:

A. You can have this.

B. It is for you.

C. In fact, it exists only because you want it.

D. So you made it.

E. And it is yours.

QED.

I am speechless after all. And, at least in our culture, what we say with our bodies is not evidence that we are saying anything at all.

2.

Alex confirms me again. There are three other girls. I sit next to Carla. She doesn't speak much English.

Where you from? she says.

Cambridge, Massachusetts.

She shrugs.

The United States, I say.

I, Brazil, she says.

How old are you? I say.

Agency tell me say sixteen. But fourteen. She shrugs again. And you?

Seventeen.

Then the hairdresser tilts her head down so he can glue extensions into the back. We stop talking. Alex comes over.

Does anyone have any paper? he says. The makeup artist rifles through his kit and hands him a notepad. A pen too? The hairdresser stops his work and finds one in his case. Alex takes it and looks at Carla. A long look. He tucks her hair behind her ear, out of her face, while he stares at her. You're so beautiful, he says. He leans against the wall and starts to draw her.

I want him to draw me. If he's not drawing me, then I'm not doing a good job. I can get cut or replaced next time. And I feel protective. She's only fourteen. Alex looks old. Maybe he's just being an artist. Maybe I'm just jealous. She looks uncomfortable. Her cheeks are red and she hasn't said a word. He touches her hair again and she lowers her eyes. I wish he were touching me. Last shoot he was infatuated with me. But I was the only girl there. Maybe I'm not his favorite. Maybe it's just how he acts with every model. He's booked me five times, but now he's brought in other girls. I'm old news, both these girls just started. At least I'm still shooting first.

The stylist brings me over to the clothing rack. Like at most shoots, everything happens in the same space, the hair, the makeup, the wardrobe. He gives me a dress to put on. There's never a place to change, so I get naked in the corner and pull the dress on over my head. It's tight. It gets stuck over my face and I try not to think everyone might be looking at me. Two styling assistants come over and help me pull it. When my head is freed I don't look up. The assistants pull the dress all the way down.

Look at that body, the stylist says.

I told you, says Alex.

Do you work out? the stylist asks me.

In, like, a gym? No. But I play soccer and basketball at school if that counts. I don't know what answer they want, but referencing school makes them laugh.

The dress is skintight. I have small boobs and a small ass, but I also have a small waist, so when I turn profile, I think I might look curvy.

After this shoot I don't see Alex for months. I ask Charlotte what happened, why he isn't shooting me anymore. Maybe, she says, it's because you're a virgin. Maybe you're too young for him.

Show season starts and I'm not booking the good shows I booked last time. They send me to Milan. I have to miss a week of school. Nobody wants to book me. Finally I get a fitting for a top show. The stylist puts me in a fur dress and I tell him I don't wear fur. He says, Then you can leave. So I get dressed and leave.

Back at the hotel one of the agents sent to Europe with us asks me to come downstairs and talk to her. She says: Nobody knows who you are, so it doesn't matter if you won't wear fur. They'll just find another girl who will. If you get famous enough later, you can make a statement. Maybe then they'll cancel the look, or put it on a new girl and it will fall into obscurity, or you can talk about it in the press. But right now you should wear it and build your career.

I wear it.

After my mediocre show season Charlotte tells me she has a plan. I can cut off my hair for two confirmed stories. I say, Let me think about it. She sends pictures. Short everywhere, then long in the front, floppy. But I guess I can always cut that off later. Mom says, Do you want to cut your hair? It doesn't really matter, I say, it's just hair.

I don't like the haircut. It hangs over my eyes, my face. My hair is too thick. I tuck it behind my ear and it looks poofy. I go to school and everyone says, Whoa. I can tell they all think it looks bad. I put bobby pins in the long part to hold it back and try to ignore what I look like. It's just hair. It's just for work. How can I complain?

I want to shave it all off, but Charlotte wants me to ride out the look she says they created for me. She asks me to take pictures of the haircut to send to clients. They don't look good. I ask her what Alex thinks of the haircut. She says she sent his office Polaroids but didn't hear back. You're not his girl anymore, she says. You shoot with other big folks now. I want to keep shooting with him more than anything else but, of course, I can't tell her that.

Finally I book another good editorial. At lunch the makeup artist tells me the photographer loves me. He does? Oh yeah, I think he has a crush big time. The second half of the day is easier once I know that.

When I talk to him he blushes. He likes being teased. We're on the beach and his foot is swollen up from a sunburn and I say it looks like a big baby foot and he loves it.

Hey, he says between shots, tapping me on the back, don't call me baby foot.

Okay, what, then?

Uncle David?

How about creepy Uncle David?

Well, you know how to make me feel like an old pervert. You better be careful or I'm going to insist you sit on Uncle's knee, like I do with all my naughty nieces.

I roll my eyes. Whatever you say, creepy D.

In May high school is over. Mom and Dad help me move to New York. I'm going to try modeling full time. Before she leaves the city, Mom says she wants to buy bedsheets. She forgets her wallet, so I pay. I'll pay you back, she says when I swipe my card. The sheets are eighty dollars.

When we get back to my new apartment, she takes the sheets out to show Dad.

You better pay me back, I joke when she hands me the price sticker she's picked off to put in the trash.

Are you crazy?

What?

Who bought your clothing and your food for the last seventeen years? Who paid for your school? You've made more than I've made in a lifetime in the last two years and now you're a greedy rich person?

I was joking, I say. Honestly I don't care. It's something you would say! You're the one who said you'd pay me back!

(How is it that I've made more than her entire lifetime earnings?)

So now you're keeping a tab for your own mother?

My face is hot. I can't believe she thinks this about me.

She turns away to unpack the sheets.

The next day Dad makes breakfast. It smells and tastes just like home, but we have no place to sit. When we finish, Mom suggests they get on the road.

They hug me at the door and I watch them go down the thin staircase. I wave again and Mom says goodbye again and I love you, and then they are gone.

Mom calls (her voice!): Should we swing back around and pick you up? You could come back home for the weekend since you're not working. I wonder, what are the rules for needing each other now?

I sense that I am supposed to stay, that I am not supposed to bother them further. I am almost eighteen, I do not need money, they cannot offer advice on fashion, and when I ask for it, they just say, Well, what do you think?

That's okay, I say, I'll stay and set up.

But the apartment is unpacked.

On Monday, since I haven't heard from her, I call Charlotte.

No bookings or options this week, she says. How about castings? It's just a quiet week, she says.

I don't have anything to do. No homework. No school. No friends. I call Charlotte every morning and ask about options. Every morning she says she doesn't have anything. I wonder if I should go home. I miss my family.

I wake up at nine. Then nine thirty. Then ten. I go out to get things for the apartment. A laundry bag, more sponges, shampoo and conditioner, a mop, a bathmat. I find a kitchen table for fifty bucks. I get toilet paper and a bamboo drawer separator and a wooden spoon, spatula, and whisk. I get magnets for the fridge. I get my own copy of *The Joy of Cooking*.

I get a rubber plug for the tub and take a bath. I get some candles to surround the tub like in the movies.

I wait until the afternoon to call Charlotte and ask about next week. I have one option and maybe some castings.

I wonder again if I should go home for the weekend. I tell myself to stay and visit museums.

The Neue Galerie is owned by the Lauder family. (They also own the famous makeup line.) Skinny White women with pink cheeks hang in all the rooms, drawn by Egon Schiele, exposed, naked, sharp lines mark the width of their hips and the arch of their backs. They have pouty lips and visible ribs, pointy breasts, and they look exactly like models. I buy the catalog.

I head downtown slowly, on foot, through Central Park. It's just a slow month, Charlotte said. Maybe I should have gone to college. But we decided it would be best to take advantage of the momentum, the haircut; you never know how long you'll last in fashion.

Mom calls and asks how I am. I tell her about the museum.

That's why people live in New York, she says enthusiastically.

Sunday night I go to a party Charlotte wants me to go to. It's for some charity. My name is in handwritten calligraphy on a place card, which I sneak into my bag. A photographer I've worked with auctions one photo sitting, a single portrait, for ten thousand dollars. I sit at a table with celebrities and nobody talks to me and my hair looks bad, but when I walk out I get a gift bag with a box set of four seasons of *Sex and the City*. At least now I have something to do.

I stay up late and watch on my laptop. I start to like nighttime. At night I'm not supposed to be doing anything, so I can just lie in bed like everyone else and watch TV and not feel terrible. During the day I worry that someone from fashion is going to see me on the street and know I'm not working. I try to walk with purpose, but I don't have anywhere to be. Sometimes I just walk quickly in a big circle.

The only work-related task I can think of is trying to get myself cooler clothes, because Charlotte is always telling me to dress better and has even taken me shopping a couple times. Just a block from the apartment I find a consignment store, all designer labels. I pick a Balenciaga sweater, a Marc Jacobs sweater, Chanel shoes, a Helmut Lang T-shirt and long-sleeve shirt, and pay almost four hundred dollars with tax. I've never spent so much money. I pull the tags off and throw the receipt out in a trash can on the street so nobody will ever see them.

Charlotte finally calls and tells me she has a contract. Big money. Big deal. But my first contract turns out to be glamourless. It's for a department store I've never heard of, but they signed Eric. He is a legend. The press call him the last male supermodel.

To close the deal I have to fly to have dinner with the client and shoot a day with them. Charlotte comes. Our plane is delayed and we sit at the gate making conversation. She takes a call. I text high school friends. They are all at college. Nobody is texting me back, but while Charlotte's in the bathroom, I figure out how I could lie to her. She's been telling me Alex and maybe lots of photographers won't shoot me anymore because I'm a virgin. So when she comes back and asks, Who are you texting? I've got a story ready.

My friend in California who goes to Pomona. Our mutual friend is visiting, it's drama.

Why drama?

Well . . . , I start, but they call our flight. I have to get the lie out now, before we board. Basically it's this guy I lost my virginity to, and now she wants to know if she can sleep with him. So awkward. I mean, I don't really care. But, like, it's so awkward. I say some more stuff I think is part of the virginity-loss-boyfriend-drama script. When we sit down she says, Wow, well, welcome to the club. I think she's bought it. She likes being the big sister/surrogate mother, and so I really get her when I say, Even my mom doesn't know. And then I pretend to be moody and look out the window because I can't answer any more questions. Then I really do feel bad because I lied about Mom.

We meet the clients in a dark hotel bar. There are four of them and they already have drinks. When we sit down, the waitress comes over and asks if we'd like something. Charlotte orders wine and then I order cranberry and vodka.

The next day is the trial shoot with Eric. Eric looks like a newscaster. He's got a quick smile, small blue eyes, blond hair, tan skin, and wrinkles on his forehead. He ma'ams and sirs and holds doors. While we're shooting he asks me: Where are you from? How long have you lived in New York? Do you like it? So, how many siblings do you have? Do you have a boyfriend?

A week later the clients are in New York and Charlotte says I

have to go to dinner with them again. We go to Mr. Chow uptown. Apparently it's part of fashion's lore, and Eric's agent is
reminiscing about all the crazy dinners he's had here. Eric is reminiscing too. The clients love gossip. I'm just laughing when they
laugh. The client sitting next to Eric says, But seriously, how
many people do you fuck a year? Eric laughs.

The client says: Eric's like, How many days in a year?

Eric laughs.

Now they're going around the table. I'm going to have to say
a number. Two, I say, and look down. They say, You're so sweet.
And I say something about my "ex."

After dinner Eric says, Who wants to go to the Dio? Everyone
starts talking about the last time, and I figure out it's a strip club.
The girls say they are in. One of the clients, a gay guy, says, Men
or women dancing?

Women, of course, says Eric. Cameron, are you in?

Eric's agent pays the bill and we all move outside. The client,
the gay one, says, I've never been to that kind of strip club. The
girls are all chatting with Eric and ignoring us, so I say, Me neither, even though he's not talking to me. He smiles conspiratori-
ally and says, Should we go? I think: When will I have another
chance? But also the idea makes me feel sick, because I'm not sure
what will be expected of me if I go. Will it be like that movie
Coyote Ugly and I won't be cool unless I end the night dancing on
a bar?

Eric leans in and says, C'mon, it'll be fun. I try to smile. The
girls are having fun, babe, it's chill, he says to me, and turns back
to his audience.

I tell Eric's agent I'm gonna go home.

He says, Are you sure? It's not a trashy place, it's just like a bar
with performers.

Next time, I say, and start double kissing everyone goodbye.

I walk away from the group saying I'll take the subway, it's faster. Instead I catch a cab around the corner so I don't have to wait with them and make more conversation.

We sign the contract. It's a confirmed six shoots over one year with an option to do my own denim line. I call Dad. I finally signed a contract, not high-profile but good money. I tell him it's almost $300K. Wow, he says, I think you might break a million dollars soon. It feels like a video game.

At the first contract shoot Eric arrives at the hotel before me and a junior client meets us both in the lobby to check us in. Eric gets his key and walks off.

He always has a woman waiting, she tells me, following him with her eyes.

Really? I look but he's gone.

Didn't you see the woman he met at the elevator?

Does he pay them, or . . . ?

He's a supermodel, he can probably call his fans.

You think?

The shoot is boring. Forty photos a day wearing plastic prom dresses, cheap suits, and shirts that rip when I lift my arms. And the studio is freezing. When Eric and I shoot together, he asks me the same questions he asked last time: Where are you from? Do you like New York? How many siblings do you have? Do you have a boyfriend?

Oh yeah? he says, nodding after everything I say.

He's supposed to stand behind me and hold my shoulders. Then we're supposed to hold hands and walk quickly toward the camera.

I love the chemistry between you two, says the photographer.

I wonder if Eric thinks I'm interesting or just an awkward kid.

I feel like I look terrible with my hair half grown out, but I let it swing forward to cover the pimples on my cheek. I don't let him stand on the side with pimples.

Let's swap numbers, he says, holding out his phone at the end of the shoot.

We're going to be doing this together for the next twelve months, and I guess it's not bad to be friends with the biggest male supermodel in the world. I imagine running for Congress and inviting him to a fundraiser. I want you to meet my friend Eric. And donors there shaking his hand and smiling like all the clients do, while I raise my glass to make a campaign plug.

Maja, a model I know, stays with me when she comes to the city for a week. The first night she leaves after dinner to shoot with Finn for a personal project. Charlotte sets it up. She gets back after I'm asleep, so I don't get to hear how it went until the next morning.

It was awkward. She shrugs. We met at his hotel room and he had me get in the shower naked and made us drinks.

That's so weird. Did you feel okay? Were the photos okay?

I didn't see them. Anyway, he invited us to drinks tomorrow. I told him we were roomies. You should come and reconnect. He shoots a lot.

Now that I live here, this is the type of thing I am supposed to do. Finn is an important photographer. I haven't seen or booked a job with him since that horrible shoot we did in Paris. I haven't booked a job with Alex either.

I wonder if they see me like Humbert Humbert saw Lolita. "A radiant child"[1] now "pale and polluted" and "hopelessly worn at seventeen." And I am almost eighteen. I put concealer under my eyes and wet my hair to make it stick behind my ears.

We find Finn at the bar in his hotel. He already has a drink and asks what we want. I say cranberry vodka and Maja orders a martini. Maja asks, If you could only pick one, which would you rather for the rest of your life: sex or chocolate? They are laughing and answering and I have to answer next, but even though I know sex is the right answer, I get caught up in not being able to lie, so I say something like "You know," and then turn red, because really I don't know.

Eventually, because it's cold and I have nothing to say, I tell them, I'm tired, I'm gonna go, and Maja says she'll come too, she has stuff to do tomorrow. The sun is gone and we cling to each other for warmth. We giggle about sex versus chocolate, and she says I'm a good wing woman. We laugh about how dumb men are. We laugh because we are teenagers and because it makes everything better.

3.

> The inauguration of the supermodel brought the transition from
> a girl who models to the 24 / 7 supermodel icon and the supermodels
> who became the quintessential glamour laborers who were never
> off duty. . . . [Models] didn't just represent products, they lived
> the life of the luxury brands to which they lent their "look,"
> inhabiting that fantasy world so convincingly that we all started
> to believe.
>
> —ELIZABETH WISSINGER, This Year's Model

Finn, remember the first time you texted? A couple days after Maja leaves you ask if I want to get a drink again. I wish she was still here, but I put on a little dress and tell myself to be confident. I've never gotten a drink alone with someone before. But I can hang, I can network. If I can't be a virgin and a supermodel, then I have to become a good actress.

You order me a cocktail and we chat. Maybe you'll book me. You tell me about a screenplay you want to write. You could star in it, you say. I let myself believe you.

The screenplay is about a girl who is homeless; she has nothing except the clothes on her back and a dog. But she's beautiful. She has dreams. A man discovers her and invites her back to his house. It's about how she makes it. It's inspired by a girl you saw sleeping on the street. You order me another drink. They are eighteen dollars each. They taste okay. I drink the second one slowly in case we split the bill.

You order another drink for yourself. And another. You have me taste it. It's hard to focus on the conversation. You are telling me about how you're working on a project with ■■■■. Wow, I say, wow, that's cool. I don't care particularly about the work they do, but it's amazing you're working with such a prestigious institution. I didn't know fashion photographers were so respected by anyone outside the industry.

You order one last drink and ask if I want another. No, I'm okay, I'll just finish this. I hold up the sip left in my glass. When you finish, you say, Well, let's go. The night is colder and I wish I'd brought the ugly sweater that didn't match my little dress. I had been thinking this was like going to a casting but at night, and I didn't realize it would go so late. I cross my arms and my hair stands up.

What shall we do now? you ask.

I don't know?

Let's walk, you say.

Okay.

We see a girl sleeping on the sidewalk. That's your character, you say, but more beautiful, obviously.

Okay, interesting, I say, even though I'm offended for myself and for the girl.

Trash trucks are out and the streets are empty. The sound of the compactors ricochets between buildings. We turn down a darker street and walk underneath scaffolding. You stop and lean against one of the poles and stop me. You pull me to you and stick your tongue way into my mouth. It tastes like alcohol and cigarettes. Your hands are warm on my back and that feels good, but the kiss is gross. It's messy and scratchy. I don't think I wanted to kiss you, but maybe I wanted to know what kissing is like? I don't say anything and let you kiss me. Then you stop and ask if I want to come back to your place.

Not tonight, I say, to be playful and flirtatious.

Okay, you say, and hail me a taxi.

You text me to say I'm a cocktease and I try to be cool and chill and say, "Sorry, I'm just tired." You text me that you're home and wish I were there. "I wish you were here," I say. "Really?" you say. "I'll come over." "No, a friend is staying over," I lie. You don't say anything. "Good night," I say. "I love you." Then I realize you're not supposed to say you love people, but everything I did was a lie and it just came out so you would still like me. I go to sleep. The next morning I wake up late and reread our messages. I feel nauseous. But I push it out of my head. A few words don't mean anything. Nobody was watching.

I call Charlotte. Any castings? Any job options on the chart?

Why don't you go do something? Travel? Visit someone?

But I moved here to work.

I can hear Charlotte typing.

I don't have anything for you right now, she says. Why don't you go to Europe for two weeks. There's a nice editorial on hold in ▮▮▮ next week, and you can do castings, meet new clients.

I go to Europe. I get in late to the model apartment. The chaperone shows me my closet bedroom and whispers good night. I text my dad to let him know I got in okay.

The problem with having a commodity body is that wherever it's being sold, your brain has to go too.

My brain has to sit on buses and subways to go to castings that are sometimes two hours apart. My brain has to ignore the math, the number of hours spent traveling to a photographer's apartment to find his girlfriend, who says, He's not in but I'll give him your card. When I call the agency to hear feedback—they are actually looking for all local girls this season, you're just too young, they decided to take lunch, you're just not right for this story— my brain has to stop me from asking whether they could have just told me that beforehand. My brain has to work with my mouth so that it doesn't say something rude when they say how-are-you? while their eyes look at their phones. My brain and my body have to form the word "Good!" And smile in case they look up.

I start to notice that my brain is learning to turn off, because waiting becomes easier to tolerate. When my brain stops accounting for the minutes, and stops observing time in the present, my body can relax. Time passes more quickly. This change scares me at first, but it makes life easier.

When I get back to the model apartment after the first day of castings, I'm exhausted but so happy not to be alone. I tell them about a jasmine tea house in Boston where Mom went and drank tea from the same leaves seven times and how the taste evolved. Me, Emma, Jess, and Irina, who I already know from a shoot, stay up late having a tea party. Irina is quiet and is like the little sister of the group. She's fifteen and giggles at everything. Soon we are all running back and forth to the bathroom because instead of seven cups we accidentally drank seven pots.

In the morning Emma and I take the same bus and she tells me about the famous guy she's dating. He's dated other models but he's really sweet. They were on the phone all last night.

Sometimes I comb through the details of what happens next to build a court case in my head, because how else can I make a story out of them? Finn, you served alcohol to a minor. You started grooming me at sixteen and called me jailbait. (Not that you were the only one.) You kissed me at seventeen. You knew, you waited, you said, Now you're legal. Or did I say that? Everyone was saying that to me after I turned eighteen. How about the text messages I sent? "I love you"? How about the casual emails? The "hey"/"hey" that made it seem like we were friendly. We *were* friendly. How do I explain what it feels like to be empty and to be nothing like myself, nothing like a self?

When you started to fuck me, that's when the silence came. Does it feel good? It feels okay. Maybe. Maybe it feels good. That hurts. It feels like maybe you know it hurts. You're using two fingers, then three. You slap me there. Is that a thing? It doesn't feel good but I am motionless. Let everything melt away so that I no longer have a mother or friends or a sister or a brother or anyone. Not a place I can go home to, not Dad, who makes me chocolate pudding when I stay up late studying. So all that's happening is the radio, the air conditioner. You try to puncture my silence with grunts. With canine jerks till the corners of the sheet pull out from under us. Luckily, I am still a virgin, no penis has been inside my vagina, so I do not have to tell anybody.

It takes some effort to breathe slowly, quietly, to feign sleep.

When you finally leave in the morning, I get out of the bed quickly. My dress is on the floor. I stare at myself in the mirror, trying to see who is there while wiping off the fog from your shower. Later you will ask why I didn't leave a note. "What would I have written?" I ask. "Xoxo?" you text back.

I get the bus. The bus takes a long time. I didn't know if it was still running last night. It would have been better to just call a car no matter how much it cost, but I was too drunk. And how do I even get a car here? I could have asked at the hotel desk. I did not know cocktails were so strong. I had already been out with you twice. But I could not read the face of the clock in the hotel lobby. When you said I could stay, I told you, Okay, but I'm not having sex with you. I felt sick. When I got into your bed I kept my dress on and you said, Don't you want to take off your dress at least? So I took it off but kept on my bra and underwear. At least the bus is warm. At least nobody is at the door when I come into the apartment, just the sound of one of the girls in her room listening to music from her computer. I lock the bathroom and take a bath. I put my head under the water and listen to the pipes.

I email my family and friends about how amazing it is here in the summer.

Were we friends? I thought you would book me on one of your shoots if I came and hung out. You don't. But that's not exactly why I was there. I was just trying to be grown up, part of the industry, confident, uncaring.

Dad asks about my face. It has been a month or maybe more since I've been home for a visit. I am getting so many pimples. I pop them. They scab. I peel off the scabs. I can't have scabs on my face and be a model. Then they get worse, and they last longer, weeks, months. I get cover-up and always have it with me. I check my face in the light before I leave the house, dabbing and blending the beige makeup as best I can. When I am out, I find bathroom mirrors to check on them. I wear scarves that cover my chin and part my hair so it falls in front of whichever side of my face looks worse. Even when the scabs heal, red and brown marks are left. I use cocoa butter at night to try to dissolve the scars and the dead-skin edges around wounds still healing. I use tweezers. I try to pull out the white pimple stalks. They bleed. I try to only let myself pick before bed.

Has Dad ever felt concerned for me before? Nobody needed to be. I got good grades, got into college, deferred for a year to make real money, had friends. We have been walking in silence when he just comes out with it, stiff. Are you okay? I'm fine, I say. Leave me alone. I walk ahead of him so he can't look at me.

I'm not working and Charlotte doesn't even have castings for me. Every day my skin is worse. I buy stinging apricot acne scrub, charcoal masks, zinc cream, clear-complexion moisturizer, toner, and powder foundation for acne-prone skin. I buy a sharper pair of tweezers.

Finally Charlotte calls. She hasn't seen me in a couple weeks, so she doesn't know my entire forehead is covered in breakouts. If she did, I don't think she'd book me for an important job. She says catalog is where the money is now. I fly to San Francisco to shoot a day for $12K.

There must be twenty pimples on my forehead alone. I squeeze them in the airplane bathroom, then wash them with hand soap to disinfect, then put some cover-up on so I don't come back to the main cabin looking like a mess. When I get to the hotel I try to squeeze a couple more, but they're all just red bumps and scabs.

I'm mortified to go to work. The makeup artist cleans off my concealer and leaves my skin red and exposed. Then he spends a long time on eye makeup. He wants everyone to see what he's working with. That's the worst part of the day. I just sit there trying to meditate for the hour the pimples are exposed. I try not to get into conversations with people when they walk by. I pretend I'm jet-lagged and close my eyes. I tell myself: Think of the money. The crew is nice enough and they don't say anything. Eventually the makeup artist gets around to covering the pimples carefully. But there are so many, you can still see the bumps under thick foundation.

I text a childhood friend to see if she's in town. Has her summer internship started? She's living in the Mission and invites me to stay over. I call Charlotte and ask to change my ticket. She's happy to; she doesn't want me back in New York bugging her for jobs.

There are penises everywhere in my friend's sublet. The saltshakers are penises, the wallpaper is penis patterned, the showerhead is a penis. The bedroom is like a greenhouse with big windows and big dinosaur-leaf plants and in the morning the sun filters down between them and through them.

My friend has gone to work and the apartment is empty.

In a recurring dream I have just before I go to sleep, or sometimes when I wake up, but mostly when I am alone, there are two things happening: nothing and complete chaos. If I'm washing dishes, water will be coming out of the faucet like loud, violent music, screaming, banging, hyperspeed, like a time warp. At the same time, my hands will be under the warm water and I'll feel serene, hovering above everything: the dishes in the sink, this morning's oatmeal gliding toward the drain, crumbs on the counter, which I wipe with the sponge methodically into a pile and then into my hand.

I don't know if I like this feeling or if I am scared of it, but it gets me hypnotized and I sink into this lucid rewiring, the ability of the brain to experience the world as both loud/quick/chaotic/ fast and slow/quiet/rotting/growing: the blood pumping and the photosynthesis of the leaves on the tree and rotating fan blades and spinning of the planets.

Light slants across the floor and I feel like a sleepwalker. How did I get here?

Back in New York Charlotte tells me: You're not a kid anymore. You don't have a kid's body. Are you saying I'm fat? I'm just saying your body is changing and this industry has rigorous standards. You should of course do what's healthy, but it's my job to tell you the truth.

Although she repeats it a few times when options get dropped, I try to put her words out of my mind. I get a summer membership to a pool and tell myself it's for my own health. I bike to the pool and then swim for as long as I can stand it. It's nice, actually. It's like meditation, except when I'm meditating on what Charlotte said. Sometimes I write after I swim and the words come pouring out.

Charlotte says, I think you should shoot some new images with Finn. Just for us, like a test, not for an editorial. Don't worry, it's not weird, a lot of girls have done it.

I don't have to be nude, right?

Of course not. The important thing is, he'll give us the photos right away, and if they look good we can use them in your portfolio. We really need new work. And you know, it could be nice to reconnect, since you haven't shot together in a while.

I'd nearly forgotten the last time we actually worked together was over a year ago. I'd seen you so many times since, but of course Charlotte didn't know that.

The call sheet says 10:00 A.M. When I arrive, it turns out you're on another job. An assistant stops me at the door to your studio and tells me to wait in an empty room down the hall. When you come in, you say the feeling is raw and intimate. No hair or makeup. You say, I know you don't do nudes, but can you just wear a towel? I say, Okay, and go behind a foam board to change.

I have fifteen minutes before I need to get back, you say when I come out.

I sit on the floor and bow my head and let my hair swing and cover my eyes. I close my eyes. I feel the blood pounding in my lips; they are hanging down, open like after crying. The corners of my eyes are wet but I look up and stare into your camera. Tilting my head so the tears don't run. I cough, pretending like I'm holding back a sneeze. Profile again, you say. Eyes closed.

Charlotte doesn't think I should take another year off school, but she says it's up to me. I'm not ending the year a supermodel. I am at the lowest point in my career. Not bad, still pulling occasional $10K day rates. But I haven't shot any big campaigns or editorials this season, or with Alex or Benjamin in almost a whole year.

I try to Polaroid myself, setting up the timer, then running backward in my underwear. I can't tell if I've gained weight. My hair is bad and my face still has pimples.

Mom and Dad come and we load boxes into our minivan. I hand keys to the apartment over to another model who will take over the lease, and press send on the email letting Wellesley College know I'm done deferring and will be coming in the fall after the gap year ends. I sit in the back of the van and text you, thanking you for the photos. Just a little more work before I get home.

4.

Mom says all presidents go to either law school or business school, so an economics major is a good choice, if that's still my plan. And I don't want to close any doors.

Economics is power. It's a way to have a conversation with someone or frame an idea that generates consensus, or at least acceptance, very quickly. It masquerades as science; it attracts people who do not want to be mired in the emotional, the historical, or the political.

Grayson, who says I don't need to call him professor, takes a liking to me. I come to his office after reading Wikipedia articles and argue for Marxism. Mostly to tease him. He sits on various boards, he predicted an economic crisis, and he answers phone calls from reporters while I sit across from him. He says, You only have to visit Cuba once to know communism can't work. A black market exists wherever there is communism, he says, so your only choice is whether you accept capitalism as inevitable and regulate it, or not.

One day I come in and he tells me he googled me and he is certain that pictures like the ones where the outlines of my nipples are visible through my shirt—and he turns his computer screen to show me the offending image—are hurting my chances of being taken seriously. You should be careful, he says. You could be a great economist.

He should have looked at that picture and understood I took capitalism seriously. The only way for a young woman to make nearly a million dollars was to accept that her highest value (in this system's accounting) was the way she looked.

He says our job as economists is to constantly ask: What results in the most equitable allocation of resources? And capitalism, he says, is the best option we have. But how do you explain my job? I ask. According to the Department of Labor, models average a little over twenty-five thousand dollars a year, far below a livable wage.[2] And that's just models; wage theft[3] and unlivable wages[4] are standard throughout the entire supply chain. He says some markets are dysfunctional and "winner-take-all" and gives me a paper, Frank and Cook (1995), about how professional athletes and rock stars are paid. In a few years, Obama's chief economic adviser Alan Krueger will argue, "We are increasingly becoming a 'winner-take-all' economy . . . [where] the lucky and the talented—and it is often hard to tell the difference—have been doing better and better, while the vast majority has struggled to keep up."[5]

I begin to understand the fashion industry not as dysfunctional but instead as a leading edge. As one of the most prolific producers of consumer goods, the industry models what rampant consumerism requires: extractive labor and environmental practices needed to keep growing, and advertising and media to make the culture of disposability both normal and aspirational.

I feel lonely. In my dreams Mom is diagnosed with terminal illness and the time we have left together is too short. I call her and decide to come home for the weekend. When I wake up, the sound of Dad turning on the shower and my sister peeing and my brother's heavy steps tumbling down the stairs feels like seeing bulbs poke up in spring. How long can I stay here?

I get good grades and fill out transfer forms for Columbia. I'm not giving up yet. Ivy League supermodel is still in the cards.

Grayson says not to take it the wrong way, but he thinks I would have been a great wife. If we had met, you know, forty years ago, before he got married, and we were closer in age. You're my match, he says.

School is over and we are getting a goodbye lunch in Harvard Square. He is retiring and I am headed back to New York. I have been laughing and pressing him to say whatever it is he was going to say. He has been asking who I want to work for after school. He knows the head of the IMF and the finance minister of Nigeria.

He is the exact person I have trained myself to impress. When I ran the Boston Marathon with just two weeks' preparation, it was Grayson who was bowled over. Smitten. He goes to the women's soccer games. He likes toughness, and still, femininity in the form of swinging ponytails and girls in sports bras. He likes endurance, and still, acquiescence, the performance of strength in a contained sport, a celebration of acceptable accomplishment, nothing threatening, just a medal for a well-bred girl, a fine specimen.

I have known his feelings all along. I have known since I stayed to help his wife clean dishes at his house after he had the entire class over for dinner, and when I finished he said he would drive me back to the dorms. I hugged his wife and got into his car and he listened hungrily to me. I teased him. He liked it. Teasing, I think, helped him imagine we were equals.

But I wanted the A. I wanted him to call Columbia and write me a good recommendation.

Later that night, at a dinner with Mom and her friends, one of whom knows Grayson from her days as a student, I repeat our lunchtime conversation. It gets back to him and he emails to say he is hurt and disappointed. He says he thought for a woman who had modeled, it wouldn't be a big deal.

I had pressed him to say it. I had been friendly the whole time knowing how he felt. I reassure him it's not a big deal.

5.

If I'm coming back to model, I want to come back powerful.

I buy Charlotte a designer bag to thank her. I've heard of other models doing extravagant things like this, and she loves fancy bags. It was seven hundred dollars. I ask her to meet me at a café, and when we sit down she won't talk. She knows.

I got you a—

Say what you're going to say.

I need to try a different agency.

So you made up your mind?

Yes.

She stands and walks out. Her tea comes and I ask the waitress for the check. My heart is pounding. I was prepared to bring up poorly negotiated contracts. I wasn't going to say, One way to refresh my brand is to change agencies. What I really wanted was to stop being the kid. I wanted to bring something to the table, my face and body, sure, but also my own network, experience, creativity, savvy, and I didn't want an agent who called me after every dropped option and suggested I might be too thin or too heavy or too virginal.

At the new agency I tell everyone I have come because I want to work with Hector. It works. It's a good ego stroke. The other agents and the owner are squirming. I know everything is about having an ally whose success can become tied with mine, and who is powerful within the agency and the industry.

Hector asks me: What do you want?

I tell him: Either I want to shoot with ███████ or I want a huge beauty contract, ideally both. I figure shooting with ███████ would be a stamp of legitimacy, a sure sign that I was part of the fashion elite. And then I could quit, carrying with me forever that I had briefly been a supermodel. And if I got a contract, I'd cash out on the only real value of continuing to work in fashion: money.

The second time I come in, I say hi to Hector first, then double kiss all the agents on the women's board hello. I wear baggy jeans because I want to say, Now, you signed me; you don't own me. I wear a shirt I usually sleep in, since an older model gave it to me from her closet when I hung out at her house last year. It's baggy and threadbare. I wear it with a white lace underwire bra a stylist gave me. I want to look like I don't care, but also sexy, cool.

When I head to the elevator to leave, the owner comes out of his office and beckons to me. Come chat, he says.

I sit across from him. He has a private office.

We value politeness here, he says.

That's great, I say.

Yes. So when you come in, you come back here first and say hi to me, ask how I am, okay? I am the owner of this agency.

Okay. I mean, your office door was closed, so I didn't know . . .

Do you know why ███████ is so successful? Or ███████?

Why?

Because they are kind, because they are good-hearted people, because when they come in they say hello to everyone.

I find it hard to even nod. The idea that models are successful because they are kind? I have seen all types of people find success, and it is not uncommon to see a famous model with harsh words for an assistant, or being dismissive and difficult while a manicurist crouches under a hair and makeup table to polish their toes. At times I have been sullen and distant on jobs—despite constantly berating myself for having any frustration, reminding myself, You said yes!—and the same clients have continued to book me.

You can go, he says, looking into his computer screen. I stand up.

Okay, have a nice day. I head to the door.

Now wait, he says, and stands up to block my way. Now, he says, we kiss goodbye. He pulls me into him in an awkward double-kiss hug.

On the street I look at my phone. I want to go home, but I am here to work. The owner would not have talked to me that way if I were powerful.

Hector calls. You know that story you shot with Isaac? We can't find any tear sheets. Do you have them?

I don't, but Isaac probably does.

Okay, let me see if someone here knows him.

I think I might have his number. I can ask?

Are you sure?

No big deal.

Maybe I should just let Hector find a connection to Isaac. When we shot, Isaac kept telling me to imagine we just fucked, or imagine he was my boyfriend. And when I glared at him he said, Okay, ex-boyfriend. But I have his number and I want to start off this relationship with Hector powerful. I have to prove I have my own relationships and I'm not a kid. They have to know they don't own me or my success. I have to show them I'm easy and capable. I text Isaac asking for the tear sheets.

"I'll give them to you if you come out for a drink tonight."

"Seriously?"

"Not on a date, just with friends. My sister is gonna be there."

"Fine," I text back.

My sublet is cold and dark, but I am grateful to be alone and unseen. I look in the mirror. Am I fatter than when I started? I can't tell. Maybe my arms are thicker. I used to be able to fit my thumb and first finger around my bicep.

When I met with other potential agents, ██████, who ran one of the most prestigious agencies in New York, told me they'd take me on if I lost 15 pounds. I'm nineteen, 5' 9.5", and 116 pounds. Losing 15 pounds would be stupid, and would certainly shorten the length of my career (and probably my life, but for the purpose of this argument, that doesn't matter). His comment made me furious and even more obsessed with what I could do to be powerful. I wanted to text him, "My lowest-earning year was still hundreds of thousands of dollars." Last year, while I was at school, while my career wasn't doing well, I still made more than many girls on his board, and I came with clients who booked me frequently. But ██████, like everyone really, was part of the game of exclusivity, and hierarchy, and controlling young women. Maybe that was good business. Last season all the models he represented walked every show and lost so much weight that there was a lot of fainting.

██████ hadn't told me to my face, of course; he told me through this other guy, who worked for him but used to be at my last agency, and even then this guy, who was willing to deliver the message, couldn't say the words out loud, so he texted me after I left the meeting: "██████ says they'll take you if you lose 15 pounds."

I wash off my makeup and put pimple cream on my pimples and cocoa butter on the ones I picked and sit on the bed and cry because I am so upset with myself for continuing to feel hurt by his suggestion I lose weight. I know a person's looks don't determine their value. I also know that they do. What does the truth matter when it's not how anything works?

I pull on a low-cut dark-green dress with a rope belt that pulls it tight everywhere. I go back to the bathroom to look in the mirror and pop a pimple on my chin. It bleeds. I put toilet paper on it. I pop one on my forehead and one near my ear. Soon I have six red spots. I lie on the bed and wrap the blanket over my legs, hoping the air conditioner's cold exhaust on my face will take down the redness. I get up and look in the mirror again; I look worse. I don't have to leave for another hour and a half. But now I can't leave early and walk around, in case I see someone. I have to wait for the swelling to go down and the open wounds to dry so I can put on makeup. I feel trapped.

Maybe I can nap for thirty minutes. I lie back down and pull the blanket over my body, leaving my face pointing toward the cold air. I set my phone alarm and fall asleep. When the alarm goes off, I get up and the redness has gone down a little. I pat powder on my chin, where the wound is still wet and the concealer won't stick. I put on eyeliner. I put my hair up but then pull out shorter hairs to cover the pimples on my temple. I can't believe I'm spending time on any of this. Now I'm going to be late. I wish I were having dinner at home. On the street Mom calls.

How are you?

Good. Headed to get a drink with this photographer and his friends so I can pick up some tear sheets for Hector. I miss you.

Why don't you come home for the weekend?

Maybe. I only have two weeks on the sublet.

Who cares? Come home for a few days.

There's a lot to do here. I still haven't found a place. I'm here, Mom. I have to go.

When Isaac walks up I remember how much I dislike him. His

unnatural tan. His crisp light-blue business shirt, unbuttoned so his chest hair and gold necklaces are visible. He smiles like a snake and holds my waist in his hands when he double kisses me.

This is my sister, Val, and her husband, Andrew.

Nice to meet you.

Shall we go in? Isaac says.

Are we waiting for anyone else? I ask.

We're all here, he says, and strides toward the door, pulling it open for me.

I am trying to smile at them, but this is a double date and he tricked me into it. As soon as we're inside, I go to the bathroom. I lock the door and it's calm for a second. A candle is burning. This is a fancy place, the bathroom is clean, not a bad place to be. I look in the mirror. In the dim lighting I look good, look sexy, I can't see any pimples. I decide I feel confident.

When I sit down Isaac says: So, are you hungry? Shall we order dinner?

Oh, I thought we were getting drinks, I say.

Do you have someplace to be? He laughs and his sister smiles like she's in on it.

I guess not, just an early day tomorrow.

Oh, you're working?

Yes, I lie. Now what if I bump into him tomorrow? I think. Do I have to stay inside all day? Maybe I can go somewhere far from lower Manhattan. Maybe I should go home.

Okay, then let's eat. He opens the wine menu. Red, white?

I don't drink.

You don't drink? And you came out for drinks?

Usually I just have tea, I say.

Well, tonight will you have some red?

Ah, no, not me. I don't drink. My uncle died of alcoholism.

(This isn't a lie. Mom tells us all the time: Alcoholism is genetic. This is what I remember: He had the same skinny legs we all did, and he wore socks pulled up to his knees and that made them look even skinnier. The way he looked at you gently, sideways, when you were talking reminded me of my brother. And he knew card tricks and always taught us one. Mom said he was good at bar games: cards, pool, shuffleboard. He was easy to be around.)

Anyhow, nobody argues with me after that. Everyone orders appetizers and first courses and main courses. Nothing is less than thirty dollars.

At 11:00 P.M. dinner is over and there is no more wine to drink, except in my glass, which Isaac poured and is still full. We are the last people in the restaurant. Isaac and his sister split the bill. I keep offering money but he won't take it.

Outside on the street I say, Okay, now you owe me tear sheets!

I don't have them on me. I'll messenger them to your agency Monday.

Then why did I have to come?

Isaac looks embarrassed, but then he says, Can I walk you home?

His sister and her husband are standing halfway down the block.

I'm fine, I say.

C'mon, let me be a gentleman. It's late. I want to make sure you get home safe.[6]

I'll be fine.

All right, well, can we do this again?

Hmmm, we'll see.

He leans in and I give him a double kiss. But he hugs me for too long. I pull away. I wave to his sister and her husband and then skip down the street, trying to get as much distance between us as I can even though I look silly.

The next day I wake up late. Almost ten. What am I going to do? By the afternoon I have done almost nothing. Finn texts me, asking if I want to go to ██████████ and shoot some photos. Maybe Charlotte spoke to him to set this up and he doesn't know I've left the agency. Before I left, Charlotte told me one prong of her strategy for me was that I could shoot new photos to kick-start a comeback.

"When?"

"About to drive up right now."

I tell myself, Be chill, hang, get new photos. This is power.

"All right."

He tells me to meet him at his car. I walk over and he's waiting next to an old convertible.

Isn't she pretty?

In front of his 1950s car he reminds me of Humbert Humbert.

I get in.

As soon as the car starts moving, I realize I have nothing to say and slump until my knees fold onto the glove compartment, then stare at my legs, not wanting to look out the window and be seen, not wanting to look at him.

Looks like it'll be about two hours there, he says.

I try to let my body relax into the forward motion of the car, let my eyes get heavy watching the buildings passing and the streets becoming highways toward a destination. I want to fall asleep. I sink lower and close my eyes. Keep going, I think, don't stop driving. The wind is blowing my hair everywhere and my pimples are hidden. I'm glad he doesn't say anything while we drive.

I wake up when we stop for gas, and the sun is low because we hit traffic and I'm cold. I didn't bring anything. He opens the trunk and offers me a sweater. It's black cashmere, soft, warm, smelling like a body. I pull it on. Thanks, I manage to say. I wonder if we are friends. If we are adult kind of friends. Like when people say you can just be silent with someone.

There's a good sushi place, he says. Want sushi?

If the sun sets, we won't be able to shoot pictures. What am I doing?

Sure, I say. I guess we'll get dinner and drinks and I can catch the bus back to the city. I can hang, it's only the annoyance of logistics I'll have to deal with.

We order sushi and he orders sake. I drink sake. What do I say? Why am I here? He asks questions and I can barely string words together. I don't recognize this person, it's almost as if I've been drugged, I just keep telling myself I can get on the bus back. He asks about where I'm staying in the city. A sublet, I manage. Where? Elizabeth Street. More sake. I don't know what time it is. I haven't even looked at my phone.

After dinner he says, Let's get a drink. Since I came all the way out here, I guess I should. Relationship building. I'll sleep on the bus. We go to a bar and get a drink. I'm drunk by then. Just like driving, and sleeping, drinking starts to feel like momentum.

But then after more drinks and more time passing, he says he wants to go. Go? Yes, I'm tired, he says. Okay, just drop me off at the bus. What? You're not going to stay? Stay where? I have a guest room. There are no more buses. Hmmm. Let me check the schedule. On my phone I look for the times. The last one is in ten minutes. It's not far from here. What? Okay, if that's really what you want. I don't know if we'll make it. We get to the car. I wonder if I'm walking funny. I guess he must not be drunk if he's going to drive. I have a guest room, just leave in the morning, we can shoot pictures tomorrow when the sun is up. That is why I came, pictures. I am drunk and the car is moving and I say okay. Okay, you'll leave tomorrow? Okay.

When we get to the house I sit outside while he turns on the lights. It's cold. He comes up behind me and wraps his arms around me, and it's just like when I put the cashmere sweater on: I feel gratitude for the warmth. I'm not dressed for the evening out here. Maybe it's big-brother-y. A bear hug. Warmth and nerves shooting through my body and I'm drunk. I ask myself, Does this feel nice? But I don't want to do anything with him. I want to be loved and held and taken care of, by anyone really, but not sex. He disgusts me. He is sloppy, his wet lips and feeble conversation. I pull away and walk to the house and say I'm going to bed. Already? You don't want a drink? We've been drinking all night. But I already opened the wine. Just take a sip at least. Two glasses are on the counter. He hands one to me. Okay, one sip. I put it down. Really, that's it? Okay, I say, and take a big sip. Where is the bathroom? I brush my teeth with my finger. I pee and then just keep sitting on the toilet, staring at the floor, for a long time after. I think I'll shower to get warm. I lock the door and take my clothes off. I don't care if he's waiting or if I didn't say I was going to shower. I turn on the water and watch a candle he lit flicker against everything clean and white. A house like a hotel. I stand under the water. I'll have to put concealer back on before bed to cover my pimples. Good thing it's in my pocket. I wonder if I'll use all the hot water. I'm wasting it. He knocks and tries the handle. You okay? Yes. Save me some hot water. Okay. I turn off the shower and dry off with a white towel from a folded pile and put my underwear and dress back on. I turn on the fluorescent mirror light and put on concealer. Am I taking too long? I come out.

Where is the guest room? Here. He leads me. Thanks. He goes back down the hall and starts to shower. I get under the covers and turn the lights off and try to fall asleep quickly. Take me to tomorrow. But it's been maybe only half an hour when he comes in. He sits on the bed. The mattress sinks. Are you asleep? Yes. He puts his hand on me. Why are you sleeping? I'm tired. We came all the way out here. So?

He says something else. He says, I can't hear you. My eyes are closed. What is going to happen next? I keep my eyes closed and he moves his weight, and this pulls the sheet tight across me and sags the bed further but I hold still. He tries to get onto the bed but it is too small. Come on, he says, frustrated, and gets up. I'm sleeping, I say. He walks to his room. I lie still and plead for sleep to arrive. He calls from down the hall. I don't answer. He gets up and comes in. This is silly, he says, annoyed with me. Then he softens. Let's at least hang out and keep each other warm, we don't have to do anything. Okay, I say. It's true, I don't like sleeping alone and I am cold. And I don't want to do anything, but maybe he gets it. So we walk down the hall to his bigger bed. I smell the alcohol on him even though he showered. It smells dangerous but also like momentum again, like something happening. His bed is warmer. And more comfortable. I get in with my back to him and close my eyes. He presses his body against my back and it is warm. He presses his erection against me. I hate how it feels. It feels needy. It feels like a whine. He massages my shoulders. That feels nice. His hands are warm. He moves his hands lower. I guess there is no one else I can do this with. His hands move to my leg. Between my legs. The alcohol and the moment and fuck it, I'm this far. He touches me. I am a sandbag. Does that feel good? I am speechless.

We don't go all the way. I won't move. Eventually he jerks himself off and it smells awful.

In the morning Mom calls and I go outside. She asks, Are you okay? You sound sick. I hear my own voice, but it sounds unfamiliar, hollow. It tastes like blood in my mouth.

I write in my notebook: "Maybe later you will say this is rape, but it's not. I chose to be here."

I lose my voice. Not to a cold, but to something else. Even when we buy sandwiches for lunch I will only be able to whisper my order. What? the woman behind the counter says. A wrap, I say, but my voice is still too quiet. While he's still inside the sandwich shop, I go outside into the sun. I cough to hear the sound of myself, to see if my voice comes back. I sit on a bench and I try to inhale, to inflate, to fill myself back up.

When Finn introduces me to a friend later in the day, I feel that he is introducing a person who does not exist. There is the idea of shame but not the feeling because I'm not there. I'm unable to make small talk. I say nothing. For the first time in my life since I was a baby, I have no idea how to speak. It's bizarre. I look at the mute self walking around and wonder where I am.

I can't get hurt. Not like Mom, anyway. Not like other women, who men attack with knives and guns. I am too tough, and too old. Nineteen isn't a child. I am tougher than any man. I can win their game and then be free to undo it. That's what I am thinking.

He takes pictures of me and says he will send them. I can use them to update my book or at least show that I have my own relationships, that I don't need an agent for every little thing. I say, There's a bus at five, and he takes me after stopping for a drink. I don't really drink, I say. My uncle died of alcoholism.

part
two

white cyc

1.

> *"Smile with your eyes," he continues, which almost finishes me off. . . . How long have I been sitting motionless in the cold? An hour and a half? Think of the money, S. You are a professional, capable of smiling seductively, with your eyes, fulfilled or about to be, there's no doubt in the minds of the audience. . . . I'm here but I'm not. I can do anything because it's not me.*
> —SUSAN MONCUR, *They Still Shoot Models My Age*

Catalog looks go: front, details, side, three-quarter, close-up, back. When I turn my back to the camera, all there is to look at is the studio's white cyc wall, which curves at the ceiling and floor so there aren't even angles to focus on, and nothing begins or ends. Occasionally the music is so loud that I can't hear the camera click or stop clicking, and when I stop posing, I'll turn around to find everyone has left.

Years pass and what's happening gives me a type of incurable sleepiness, an anxiety-induced speeding up of hours and days and months, a removal of self, where things occur around me but I feel I cannot affect their happening. Like a dream where even the surreal can't awaken lucidity. Like if a man growing in place of a plant, his bald head emerging through cracked earth, starts to beg for water and you're holding a bucket you seem only able to choose to pour or not. You cannot choose to return to your childhood home with its big beat-up couch and afternoon sun.

I begin writing for myself because I feel so inarticulate, because I have spent so much effort not remembering, not putting into words what I was experiencing, that effort had been replaced with habit, and my thoughts are muddled and I am confused about the decisions I am making.

I'm staying at the Sunset Tower Hotel in LA for work and I feel too depressed to eat. I pick up the phone and order truffle fries anyway. They come hot, with grated Parmesan on top, so of course I finish them all. Wealth makes the world greasy and easy. Black cars and room service, and people you don't have to trust or even like and who don't have to like you.

Like sitting in front of the camera, when I start to edit, I struggle to present a story of self that is legible and also more than just a reflection of the thoughtless ways we hold one another's attention.

In modeling, the body is my tool; in writing, the story is my tool. Like the model body, the story humanizes and is also entirely manicured. Cynthia Ozick compared the essay to a warm female body. See: "She: Portrait of the Essay as a Warm Body." Yet the feeling I most strongly associate with modeling is cold.

1. Shooting for next season: forty swimsuits on the beach in Miami on a day it's forty-eight and overcast, the makeup artist coming in between every shot to lipstick over my purple lips.

2. Being told not to wear a robe or jacket to avoid wrinkling the clothes.

3. Standing naked and covered in goose bumps while the makeup artist applies fake tan in the courtyard of the hotel before the sun rises. The hotel owner watches.

4. Shooting on boats.

5. Shooting on a glacier in heels and a sundress while the crew wears snowsuits and metal crampons over boots.

6. Shooting at night.

7. The art director telling me she really needs me to jump into a freezing lake in November for a shot. Production brings blankets and tea to set.

8. Wearing lingerie surrounded by giant fans to make the hair blow just so. Are the fans really making the hair look better? Well, mostly they're for the nipples, the hairdresser jokes.

9. Wearing swimwear in an air-conditioned studio, the crew spraying/pouring/throwing water so I look wet.

10. Shooting in a miniskirt in the snow.

Can a story be a cold body? Detached and uncomfortable? In photos I always appear warm.

Feeling powerless encouraged me to push words into pre-existing narratives: Mom's, fashion's, a girl's coming-of-age. Although they explained events, these stories would quickly become the same one I was always trying to escape: that rite-of-passage victim narrative our society had created for girls as we went through, or performed, our transformation into straight cis womanhood. An observation it took me years to make but that so many queer writers saw clearly and described succinctly:

"Reese spent a lifetime observing cis women confirm their genders through male violence."[*]

And

"Look to high schools, where sex education teachers are still training girls in how to relate to themselves as (inevitably straight) sexual victims and gatekeepers and to boys as sexual agents and predators."[†]

These stories were a way for White women like me to access a certain type of attention and authority. Does the need to appear perfect and innocent keep me safe or keep me speechless? I need to undermine this impulse I have to perform.

I call Mom from the set and, for the first time, I start to complain. You wouldn't believe what the location manager said to me in front of the crew . . . called me heavy for a model . . . told me

---

[*] Torrey Peters, *Detransition, Baby* (New York: One World, 2021), p. 57.
[†] Jane Ward, *The Tragedy of Heterosexuality* (New York: NYU Press, 2020), p. 13.

I looked better in the first outfit that wasn't so tight. I whisper a torrent of petty grievances into my cellphone a safe distance from the shoot, where everyone is sitting at folding tables having lunch. I tell her of course I'm grateful for the job. And she says: You should stop, do something else. You can do anything else, the world is your oyster. She tells me not to tell anyone, but when she moved to the United States for college, after living in North Africa for most of her childhood, she worried she wouldn't be exceptional anymore. Wouldn't be beautiful, wouldn't have brown hair that got called blond and complimented everywhere she went. Wouldn't be the American daughter of a diplomat, so well-spoken, so well-read. Wouldn't be wealthy, would be broke and middle-class. What I hear is: In the United States, she worried because she wouldn't be the only White girl. But guess what? she says. That didn't happen. It turned out I was exceptional, would be exceptional anywhere I went. You are one in a million, she says. You're my mom, I say. When I hang up I feel sick that this could be why I still work in fashion.

Years pass and each day I become less of a witness and more of an accomplice.

I find out at the end of the day that the client is going to use my images for a campaign in the Latina market. Why didn't you hire a Latina model? I ask. The art director shrugs. At a casting for a beauty contract they ask me, Do you speak Spanish? A bit, I say, and speak a few sentences. Is anyone in your family Latino? No, I say. Well, the tagline for the campaign is "Latina like me," so we'll have to see if we can work something out. I'm definitely not right for that, I say. We'll talk to your agent, they say. I shoot a fragrance ad where they do a take first on me and then on a Black model, who watches the clip they chose and then repeats the performance. For different markets, they say. My agent says they are paying her less than they pay me. A possible contract comes up. They want you to be the main girl, says my agent, but they want a diverse group cast. My agent runs through a rate structure where I make the bulk of the budget. Does this sound good? she asks. We can pull a group together and you can make your rate. I say: It sounds unfair. But, she says, you wouldn't do it for less, right? Right, I say. On set one day the White male photographer asks me how I can call the industry racist. Well, take your job, I say. In the last decade I've only worked with—I count on my hand—four photographers who weren't White. It's the first time I've counted. Only four! I repeat. So? he says. You're White. When it comes time to shoot the cover, they say they are going to try a double with the other model, then a single on me. The other model is young and this would be a big break. She is a Black woman and they almost never feature a Black woman on the cover. When we shoot the double she is stiff, and I see quickly that they are going to move on. I'm not sure exactly what I could do to change the situation, but I know I could ease the set, I could hold her hand and help her move into a better position. But I pause. A single cover of this publication is a big deal. I've waited a decade for it. And then, while I do nothing, they stop the shot, say it's not working, and move on to the single cover with just me, which is the one that will end up running. The casting agent is trying to sell me to the client for their runway show. She tells them: She's from Boston, she's as American as it gets, she's your thoroughbred. They laugh, I smile, and they nod. Yes, let's get her in a look.

In Michelle Cliff's "Notes on Speechlessness" she writes, "Speechlessness involves self-denial . . . to choose to express/to choose to express anger."[1] I add in the margin: "and for me, to choose to express joy/to choose to feel/to choose to feel pleasure," because both disappeared when language disappeared. I neglected life-sustaining joy because survival seemed guaranteed.

Language is insufficient. Something about it draws the finger to the scab.

"The process of making art," writes Rebecca Solnit, "is the process of becoming a person with agency, with independent thought, a producer of meaning rather than a consumer of meanings that may be at odds with your soul, your destiny, your humanity."[2]

I like that. But for me, writing feels like being forced to acknowledge that voice is created by the body and is as physical and mysterious as sneezing or cumming, as handwriting or hallucinating, and intuition isn't about choice, but something much more complex that arises from an ecosystem impossible to discover or contain, only available to experience. In writing I find out: We are only ever co-authors.

2.

Hector emails me porn. Naked women in a circle squirt water out their assholes, the video file entitled "La Fontana de Trevi." So when the hairdresser shows me "Cake Farts," a video of a woman farting on a cake, I email it back to Hector. I'm not interested in being the kid again. I'm tough enough to take whatever nonsense he throws my way. "I'm forwarding this to ███," he replies. "He loves kinky girls."

At dinner Hector asks about who I'm dating. I'm not dating anyone, but I make up stories. A real man did give me his number the other day at the bike store, so I just tell him we slept together. His name was Malik. Hector says, Once you go Black, you don't go back. I roll my eyes at him. Don't worry, he says. I'm with you, I love Black boys.

His performances remind me of what psychologists say about children acting out and testing grown-ups, that they just want to know if you'll still love them. He tells me he's best friends with the girls he books. He and ███ share a therapist. So I know everything about her, he says winking. I'm not sure if he's telling the truth, or if that matters to him, so I decide it is okay to lie whenever we talk. Every joke, laugh, blush, story from my personal life will be tailored to him and I will stay protected, anonymous. When he emails me a call sheet, he always writes, "Have fun!" And I always email him back something like "Thank you so much for another wonderful booking."

One day on set everyone is laughing about a website called RateMyPoop.com. I email him some of the photos and he replies, "How did you know this is my favorite website?" He emails me an attachment that I don't open.

After a shoot wraps, I rent a little house at the top of a hill and up a steep set of stairs in Los Angeles. I cancel jobs. I stay for two weeks by myself. Turning down work to choose writing makes me feel like I have to disprove or dismantle capitalism; otherwise what am I doing? An agent emails: They're ready to pay even more. No. Where do I fit when I make this kind of decision?

More words stick to me.

I print Michelle Cliff's essay "A Journey into Speech" and leave it next to my bed.

[I wrote] shorthand—almost—as memory and dream emerge; fast, at once keen, at once incomplete. I was also, in those sections, laboring under the ancient taboos of the assimilated: don't tell outsiders anything real about yourself. Don't reveal *our* secrets to *them*. Don't make us seem foolish, or oppressed. Write it quickly before someone catches you. Before you catch yourself.[3]

I read more. "If I Could Write This in Fire I Would Write This in Fire" and *Claiming an Identity They Taught Me to Despise.* Cliff's words are changing me. Maybe because she was coming out of a PhD program and needed to shed the rules of Western academic writing like I do. Or because she was interrogating colonialism, and the fashion industry colonizes women's bodies. Or because her words don't just slice through White supremacy, imperialism, hetero-patriarchy, enlightenment, and success: She makes words drop, swoop, swarm, sting, and then wrap around me like a diver until, even if the sun is bright on a cloudless day, it is like we are at the bottom of the ocean in the shade together, the pressure of the water and the quiet bearing down.

At the Gucci store Hector tells me my tits look great. We're there buying a dress for me to wear to a meeting with a potential client. He says it loud and in front of the salesclerk and then looks at Aimee, a younger agent, and asks her, Don't they? Great tits. Aimee looks uncomfortable. I look away.

Since Hector is selling my tits, he is allowed to say it. He says it on the phone to clients, photographers, and friends. His job is to sell my body. He's one of the few people who knows exactly how much the tits (and all the other parts combined) can be worth, and it's ridiculous. We are crude in an effort to trivialize the superficial while having our fortunes so intimately tied to it. And then there is the fact that I am the owner of these parts, and he is not, and he will make a cut of the sale, but I will make more of it, and I can leave with my body and his job is to convince me to stay. Then again, he will continue to work, and has multiple clients, and my value will diminish as I age. So it is an uncomfortable relationship between me and him and my body.

One day on set the lights make my eyes water so much that between every shot the makeup artist holds Q-tips to them to prevent tears from spoiling the look. The photographer comes and adjusts my chin with his hands. Head like this. No, head like this. No, head like this. Don't move. Then they turn up the fan to blow cold air on the hair, which makes my eyes water more. They blast music. Photo assistants hold bounce mirrors, and the flash goes off. Then everything gets turned off, but I am instructed not to move, and in silence they all look at the monitor. This goes on for hours. My neck hurts.

When I wake up the next morning I can't see. A friend comes over and says the whites of my eyes are bright pink and takes a picture. We email it to Hector and he replies, "Use eye drops." After an hour I can see but everything is blurry. I call Hector, but Aimee answers and tells me he's busy. The flash damaged my eyes, I tell her. I knew the lights were too bright. They shouldn't be using lights like that, she says. I'm going to call the photographer's studio right after we hang up and let them know. In the afternoon Aimee calls me back. Is everything still blurry? she asks. Yes, I tell her, nearly crying. The eye drops didn't help. What if the damage is permanent? What if I go blind? This is unacceptable, she says, but I did some research and I think the flash burnt your eyes and they're going to be fine. Put an ice pack on them, and if they don't get better we'll go to the hospital tomorrow. The next day my vision is back to normal and I decide I'll try to speak only with Aimee from now on.

I start to stockpile words like weapons.

The members . . . were primarily White and affluent; somehow they believed that racism and misogyny marked them as
rebels rather than merely the latest recruits to an entrenched
old guard.*

In a dream I am being pursued. I run across a Vegas casino
floor, dodge between tables and around machines. It's late and
the crowd is thinning. A waitress nods at me. I tackle the man I'm
after in a back corner and push us to the floor. Out of view, behind a deserted pool table, I straddle him and spit a box cutter
into my hand. Gripping it between my thumb and index finger, I
begin. First I slice his eyes with my hand clamped over his mouth.
He tries to bite. I slice his throat, and blood pours from between
his lips, bubbles through my fingers. Then I cut him everywhere,
dozens of slices. The blade is slippery but I grip it hard. Blood is
up my arms. I walk out, leaving the corpse. The waitress must
have done something on my behalf, because everybody pretends
not to notice me. I wake up.

Sharing our dreams is one of the most verbal ways we can
share our bodies. You have been inside me now.

I keep my words carefully like this, tucked between my cheek
and my gums: "infantilize," "colonize," "objectify," "racist," "misogynist," "harassment," "dumb." I want them to slice various
people open so that something bleeds out of them. Bloodletting.
I find places to pick my skin where nobody at work will see.
Under my hair is good.

An hour outside Atlanta for a job, we drive up to the location
and the production assistant points at some rubble in the woods
and tells me: That used to be slave housing. Then he points where

we're headed and says, And the same White family still owns the big house. The woman who answers the door tells us this again. The plantation has been in my family for hundreds of years, she says. It is the first thing she tells us, and she says it with pride. I sit on the porch waiting for the team to set up. How different is what we're doing? Celebrating this place, celebrating my White face over and over while women of color make, pack, ship, and sell the clothes for nothing close to a livable wage.

They call me to change. White bridal lingerie with one lace garter next to a bed upstairs. The bed looks old, and I start to feel sick thinking about what might have happened here. The photographer asks me to look happier. (It is unprofessional to think about rape.) Everyone on the team is European. Maybe they don't know the history? I smile at the lens. A little light in the eyes, the photographer says. I open them wider.

The next day is fall fashion outside. They walk me to an old wooden swing hanging from a tree. The production assistant I drove in with holds my arm while I make my way across the soggy earth in high heels. Do you think those were for horses? I say, pointing at two metal poles in the lawn, trying to make conversation. Or humans, he says, and laughs. I want to say something but we are on the set and the photographer is already telling me to sit on the swing. Happy, he says, grinning at me. Then he tells me to start swinging. I close my eyes and try a closed-eyes smile. I try to meditate. Focus on my breath. Eyes open, says the photographer, smile with the eyes.

3.

Finn wants me for a big job. Declining would be unprofessional. I go. Two days on location.

After work we go for a run. Nobody else from the crew wants to come. So it's just the two of us. On the way back I say, I'm worried about you. Why? Because of your drinking. You don't have to worry about me, he says, looking away, but that's sweet.

When he texts that night, I say I can't come to his room. "Just come hang out," he says. I don't reply. We have another shoot day tomorrow. "How is Finn?" texts Aimee. "You know," I reply. "Yah," she writes. "He's gross."

I spend time wondering if his parents didn't love him. Or if he doesn't have a mother, because he never mentions her. Or maybe it's fashion that makes people sick.

Finn texts me when I'm on the way home. "What are you doing?"

I text back: "I've been writing. Wanna hear a bit?" "Yah," he says. I text him: "He tried to puncture the silence with grunts. With canine jerks till the corners of the sheet pull out from under us."

I want to know if he'll recognize himself. He says, "what happens next?" I say, "nothing." He says, "can we make something happen?" I say, "I think you manipulated me." Because he is the only one who knows what happened, I think he is the only one with words for it. He texts back, "you manipulated me ;) I thought I was in love."

4.

It became very hard to think outside the fashion world once I was embedded in it and wanted to be the best.

—GRACE JONES, *I'll Never Write My Memoirs*

Gloria Steinem, no matter how old or accomplished she becomes, is still introduced as the woman who went undercover as a Playboy Bunny in the sixties. In an interview with Geena Davis about playing the president in her show *Commander in Chief,* the host reminds the audience she was a model for ████████████. I know these things, so I decline to even attend the ████████████ casting for years. But now I say yes. There are lingerie pictures of me across the internet already. And at this point the choice really is whether I will be known as a model or supermodel.

Are you sure? says Aimee, when I tell her I will do it. ████████████ is a whole different game. It'll be seen by millions of people.

When the day comes, lots of girls bring their daughters. Bill, the gray-haired man in charge, picks them up and bounces them in his lap. Aren't you pretty? Just like Mommy. His stomach presses against his button-down, tucked tight under his belt. Are you a little angel in the making? he asks them.

All the girls spend time chatting with him. Did you get my text? he asks ████. Yes, she says, and winks. I keep my distance. He drapes his arm around a girl. He rubs a girl's thigh while they speak, friendly.

There's one girl who is six inches shorter than everyone else and twenty pounds heavier. I am sitting next to ████ watching her walk. She whispers to me between sips of turmeric ginger juice cleanse, How'd she get here? Did she fuck ████████? I don't say anything. I know on his Instagram he shares pictures of dinner dates with teenage models. She points at another model and tells me she's here because she's dating one of the photographers.

At rehearsal we all come in our own clothes. We are watching ██ walk now. The nipple of one of her newly enlarged breasts comes out from under her loose tank top at the end of the runway. The girls start calling her name, laughing, cheering, whistling, and pointing to her chest. She looks down, giggles for the cameras, and covers herself.

We know what we are selling. Doesn't that make it okay? Perhaps the real problem is the exchanges outside of a contract. All the flirting, the casual nudity, the dinners, the texting, all before anyone gets paid. It's off-the-books, unregulated. I doubt many of the girls want to touch these men or show them their tits, at least not for free. But it's the only way in. Every gatekeeper expects it. Even for me, sitting here in a long, baggy dress, with other job options if I sought them out, when Bill walks by and says, So glad you're here, we double kiss, and I hug him and thank him, and our bodies press up against each other, and I smile. Or is the real problem that by participating in our own objectification for a large audience, we participate in making it difficult, or impossible, for anyone to escape being valued, or devalued, based on how they look?

Around 5:00 P.M. the camera flashes shift to two of the girls who have taken off their robes and are climbing up onto the makeup table. They're both wearing matching brand lingerie. They walk between the mirrors like the table is a runway. Did everyone wear ████████████████ underwear today? Did they buy it themselves? Was this planned, or did they just decide to climb up? It is difficult to understand what is a paid performance and what girls are choosing to do, and also what choice even is.

I'm not eating before the show; none of the girls are. Or they're making a whole show of taking a sandwich and a dessert and a pile of pasta salad, and then throwing it away when nobody's looking. Since being confirmed for the job I've been running, biking, doing Pilates, doing a spin class before call time or after work and two classes back-to-back on days I'm free. It's been a month. It hasn't felt unhealthy—actually, I feel great—but I know why I'm doing it and that makes me sick. I definitely don't want to be the only girl who looks big when the pictures come out. Hector told me he and ▮▮▮▮ were sending each other close-up pictures of cellulite on ▮▮▮▮▮'s ass they found on the internet after the last show.

Before the show starts, Bill gives his pep talk. You are the most beautiful women in the world, he says. You're more special than NFL players. Do you know why? Because there's only ever been three hundred of you! The girls cheer for him. Some look like they really believe him, but I can't tell.

The song starts for my section. And then I'm turning onto the runway and I'm full of energy. My heart is being forced onward by the bass, vibrating the stage and all my organs. I feel the eyes on me. I feel my little body working. I know how to do this: Find the smile, chin up, imagine the confidence. Swinging, stomping, left, right. Stop at the end. Shove a hip out. The air-conditioning is on, fans are blowing my hair. We're all in underwear, why aren't we freezing? I smile. I walk faster. I'm almost naked in front of all these people. They see my breasts pressed up, positioned, propped. Last night I leaned my phone on a chair and filmed myself walking in underwear to see what it looked like. How much would the camera see? They see my ass. My bikini line, waxed and smooth. My abs, lotioned, tanned, highlighted with a shiny stick. I see the other girl, she turns the corner into the light, and she winks at me. I turn off. I'm panting. Only two hundred yards at most, was I sprinting? Did I forget to breathe?

A camera is there. A production man gives me his hand to help me down the steps. Wasn't that the best high of your life? he asks. I smile.

Then the finale. Start laughing. Now go out onstage. Music so loud it's okay being nearly naked. Smile at the girls next to you and squeeze their hands. The lights are following us. They told us to dance when we got out onto the stage. Balloons drop from the ceiling. The thigh muscles, the groin, the abductor that's working overtime in heels. Feel it pulling, stretching when I stop and lean and pop the ass. Feel like laughing, feel like exploding, feel the energy like confetti, manufactured, paper-thin.

I call Mom when I leave. You're a spy, she says. Is she trying to tell me that I am not like all the other people who make this show happen? Aimee meets me for late-night sushi. She asks: How was it? And then she says the same thing: You're a spy for us. Who is us? What is a spy without training or purpose, without the equipment needed to gather evidence, without knowledge of laws or of what constitutes proof?

In the cab home I search on my phone: What is the age of consent? What is the definition of sexual harassment? What happens if you turn someone in for tax fraud? But those are just the obvious crimes. Where are ███████████ garments made? Used to be made-in-the-USA by prison labor, the results say. But not anymore; once they were found out, they moved production abroad. But did the price change? All I have is notes on my phone and a shitty voice memo of Bill's goofy speech.

I shower off the glitter and the brown body makeup, and the water at my feet turns gray. How brown did they make us? How many hands helped apply and reapply the makeup, how many other bodies covered in lotion and makeup and glitter did I press against? I wash my body a few times and use a second washcloth after the first becomes discolored.

5.

I begin to read every model memoir I can find. I want to know what happens to models when we find ourselves, no longer fourteen and doe-eyed like the day we were scouted, but adults, navigating access to mainstream media and wealth, largely made possible by poverty wages and resource-intensive production. Gisele Bündchen wrote: "A lot of the time being a model made me feel torn and guilty . . . [but] it was a work opportunity that appeared when I was very young, and I took it.[4]

The books teem with repetition.

Describing her career, Ashley Graham explains, "[One of the] unspoken rules to being successful in the industry . . . You have to be ready to do anything."[5] I had written about how often I heard the same compliment: "This girl is amazing. She'll do anything." Naomi Campbell included praise from model agent Carole White: "Naomi . . . she has no boundaries."[6]

In a used copy of Dorian Leigh's book where the pages are brown and the spine's glue cracks, I skip to the glossy centerfold where the photos are. Although she is well known in fashion as one of the first supermodels, I didn't know her name until I researched model memoirs and found hers: *The Girl Who Had Ev-*

erything. There she is, in 1947, in black and white, lying on her side in a group shot by Irving Penn that looks exactly like—and must have been the reference for—a shoot I did sixty-two years later. I search for the image I was in and find it immediately. There I am, just like her: on the floor in the front row in the right-hand corner, wearing a black V-neck dress. I didn't know her and yet I mimicked her pose almost exactly. Browsing her book I find dozens of other reproductions.

In the moments before escaping an attempted sexual assault, Leigh remembers, "Yes, of course I knew what was happening, but I wasn't exactly opposed to it."[7] And I hear my own words, "I don't think I wanted to kiss you, but maybe I wanted to know what kissing is like?" And then I hear Marilyn Monroe: "Occasionally I let one of them kiss me to see if there was anything interesting in the performance. There wasn't."[8] In my notes our stories begin to blur, and I can't remember which words are mine or hers or someone else's.

Even after I stop recording all the repetitions, I find the same words haunting the books. "Perfect," for example, appearing 163 times in Janice Dickinson's memoir, 79 in Grace Jones's, 43 in Brooke Shields's, 42 in Crystal Renn's, 39 in Pat Cleveland's, 17 in Emily Ratajkowski's, 13 in Waris Dirie's, and 10 in mine.

I copy a page from *I Am Iman* into my phone and reread it often. She captures the duality of fashion: that it privileges and oppresses. She articulates her complacency, her objectification, and the systemic effects of colonization and racism:

> I participated in the fabrication about being discovered [by photographer Peter Beard] in the bush of Kenya's Northern Frontier District. But in retrospect, I was very uncomfortable with the African Princess/Jungle Bunny myth. I

found it both sexist and racist. My silence made me an accomplice. I have always regretted that.

The white magazines considered me "exotic," like some
fruit. And the black magazines considered me not "ethnic" enough, like some head-wrap. Both of them treated
me like an object rather than a human being. This, I
learned, is the no-man's land inhabited today by blacks the
world over. We started off being branded; now we brand
ourselves. This is, of course, a classic effect of disempow-
erment and a colonized self-image. . . .

As a political science student, I understood. . . . I viewed
everything as a political statement.[9]

I am surprised to find Iman's incisive critique. I didn't know
there were supermodels who spoke like this. What magazine
writers, casting directors, and agents always seem to sell about
me is that I am an exception. Beauty *and* brains. The more I read,
the more I realize I am not an exception. And instead of feeling
diminished or quotidian, I begin to feel less alone, and begin to
sense that what modeling is and what it could be is much bigger
and broader than I thought.

The climax of Waris Dirie's autobiography, *Desert Flower*, is
when she's interviewed by *Marie Claire* and, instead of talking
about "all of that fashion model stuffs [that's] been done a million
times," she tells a "real story."[10] The article about her experience
of circumcision is published, and she helps to ignite a global
debate—being interviewed by Barbara Walters, speaking to the
UN General Assembly, and serving as a UN Special Ambassador
for the Elimination of Female Genital Mutilation. Alek Wek

writes that being able to have "a voice" to bring attention to devastation in her home, South Sudan, and work with the U.S. Committee for Refugees Advisory Council, made "being a model worthwhile."[11]

Echoed across decades and recorded in thousands of pages of text are all the ways the personal is political. But for me the personal still feels impersonal. I have been refusing to sit with the intimacy of it, giving in to the assumed meaninglessness of the work of modeling, the farce of disposability upon which the industry relies. Every shoot is always just this one day/just this crew/just this shot, and so each is easy to dismiss and difficult to change.

tableau vivant

1.

My grandmother tells me she wanted to model when she was nineteen but her dad wouldn't let her. What part of modeling did she want? If she had found success, so much might have been life-changing—the money, the travel, the independence, the fame—but I'm wondering about the act itself. What was so interesting about being in front of the camera?

She can't hear me when I ask. I say it louder: Why did you want to model?

She giggles.

Sometimes being photographed was a liberation. Plato, Descartes, and other dualist philosophers argued the mind is rational, while the body is, at best, a tool. This construction has been used as a justification to exclude and demean women, and all those deemed too corporeal, emotional, and (therefore) irrational. A model can undermine long-held binaries—body/mind, subject/object, self/other—to which the patriarchy has clung. In front of the camera we are fleshy, fallible bodies, muscles, skin, fat, and bones. We can be made into objects yet remain subjects in conversation. A photograph, which requires us to give something of ourselves up to the interpretation of another, makes it obvious that we belong to each other.

While I was researching models, Virginia Oldoini—known as the most photographed woman of the nineteenth century—caught my eye. Unlike me, Oldoini paid for each shoot, so I hoped she might tell me why modeling was interesting. What about it interested her?

She first found herself at Mayer & Pierson's photo studio at nineteen. She had arrived in Paris a year earlier, in 1855, sent by her cousin who was a minister to the king of Sardinia. The cousin instructed her to convince Napoleon III to support Italian unification and "succeed by whatever means you wish—but succeed!"[1] She became Napoleon's mistress. Reunification was announced four years later, and historians rate her contribution anywhere from conceivable to debatable to even narcissistic. What isn't debatable is the trove of nearly five hundred photographs Oldoini commissioned Pierre-Louis Pierson to take of her over the next forty years.

In Oldoini's photos, she dramatizes scenes from her own life, takes risks in performing gender, sexuality, class, and mortality, and finds ways to experiment with surrealism and deconstruction: isolating body parts, most famously looking through a hole in a frame. Yet her work is largely remembered as self-obsessed, her motivation generally reduced to a woman "fascinated by her own beauty."[2] But I recognized her effort, similar to the project of this book: an endeavor to lift the work of modeling from assumptions of superficiality to its own complicated form of labor that challenges its workers to find creative ways to co-author with an audience, limited by what our bodies can perform, what can be seen, and what can be understood inside a frame—a labor of compromise.

2.

The private me was Gisele, but the model Gisele was her. That's what I called her, too—her. She was an actress. A performer.
— GISELE BÜNDCHEN, *Lessons*

To prove Oldoini's authorship of these photos, many writers produce the evidence of her handwritten notes on negatives and test prints for gouache retouchers or paper cut to show how a shot should be trimmed. They find preliminary sketches and detailed shoot plans inside fragments of her diaries. When I begin to read about her, I too am curious about what documentation remains of her creative intentions. And I am disappointed by my need for it. Why assume that on one side of the camera sits the author of the photo, the artist, while on the other I so easily conflate the subject with their two-dimensional representation, nothing more than an unthinking object unless proven otherwise? How can pressing a shutter require more skill than the continuous performance one must create if they do not control the timing of the release?

Oldoini was the daughter of a diplomat; I was raised by the

daughter of a diplomat. Trained to see both sides, to find grace, to find it easier to be agreeable.

Mom tells me that, when being considered for a new post, her dad—who would be paid and hired—and her mom—who would be unpaid and also have a list of responsibilities to fulfill—would both be evaluated. I ask Mom what the difference was between the diplomacy her dad did and her mother's feminine labors. Mom says diplomats have a purpose, usually to further the interests of their nation-state. What is the purpose of feminine labor? I ask her. I suppose it is simply expected. But aren't there ends? Things we want to achieve? Sure, she says, sometimes.

The first time I tried to make something from behind and in front of the camera, I adopted all the usual adman strategies for a different end. I was twenty-two and had been a model for six years when the climate organization 350.org put out an open call for media explaining that 350 was the number of carbon dioxide parts per million in the atmosphere deemed safe. I saw an easy opportunity. It was 2009, we were at 390, and a group of models could "shed" these carbon parts symbolically and seductively in a comical forty-garment striptease. I wrote a short script, found a crew, and, with Aimee's help, organized a dozen models to join me in giggling and undressing on camera. All of us were White, mostly very skinny, in our late teens and early twenties, and the ad went viral. They played it on Fox News.

I cleave myself in two: an author conceiving of myself as an object.

I go back to staying quiet in public as a model. I continue developing multiple identities. I am a college student and I go to Occupy with my friends. We stay up late debating politics and economics; we share books, quotes, ideas. When I leave a working group one evening, I see a missed call from the agency and have the dissonant experience of going from talking about the 99 percent to asking how much the client is going to pay and for how many days. When Black Lives Matter protests happen in Boston, I meet friends in front of the prison and we march toward the highway at night. Days later, I am back in New York on set when the stylist tells the other model, a Black woman from Los Angeles, to take off a pair of jeans and give them to me. When the other model walks away and I put the jeans on, the stylist says, That's much better, they looked ghetto on her. I am quiet. I mean, she says, everyone looks good in different things.

By 1863 Oldoini had moved away from Paris to Passy and was rarely seen at social events. She was invited to take part in a *tableau vivant*, a private party where the audience expected she would be wearing a revealing dress. She had caused a stir previously by baring her shoulders, arms, breasts, thighs, ankles, and feet. Knowing the audience's expectations, she came ready to reveal herself . . . entirely covered in a nun's habit. She later reenacted the scene in an 1863 photo, *Ermitage de Passy*.

My first attempt to speak publicly about modeling is not unlike Oldoini's entrance. I wear a tight black dress that barely makes it over my ass and eight-inch platform heels, and I teeter onto the TED stage. Behind the scenes, a woman who is supposed to introduce me does a double take and checks, You want to be introduced just as a model? before passing her duty off to her cohost, who embellishes my bio in his introduction. Onstage I immediately change, not into a nun's habit, but into a wrap skirt that hits midcalf and a baggy button-down sweater. I step into flats. I talk about Whiteness, beauty, privilege. I know which expectations to meet, which to subvert. The talk goes viral. Top ten, then top five most viewed TED talks. Forty million views. I told a story about the undue media attention I received, and in response, I received more attention. Everything I thought fashion could bring me appears overnight: publishers and agents soliciting my first book, magazines contacting Aimee for a cover story, and what feels like every major TV network wanting to interview me. The biggest ad campaigns confirm, conferences from Japan to Texas to Australia invite me to speak for as much pay as a modeling day rate.

Now, momentarily, I am the most public voice for my profession. It feels like power. It feels like writing my own story. Except once I go off script, I don't know what to say.

I never talk about modeling. Modeling is being silent in public. Even with friends who ask, How was your day? The most I say is, I can't complain. I try never to even think about it. When modeling made me feel like crying, I told myself, Don't let this job get into your head. When it made me feel like skipping a meal, I told myself, Don't let superficial evaluations affect you. When it made me feel confident and creative and joyful, I told myself it was all too fake and exploitative and ephemeral for those feelings to be real if I investigated them. When I sold impossibly cheap clothing, too cheap to pay people well, I thought, But what can I really do? and assumed I'd be in a similar position at any number of other jobs. It made me ignore my body, like when I was wearing booty shorts in zero-degree New York winter and a space heater burned my leg and I didn't notice until the end of the day when I went to pull on my socks. When a photographer grazed my breasts, when a client watched me change, when it made me ignore my strength because it wasn't as valuable as my flexibility, I ignored so much of myself that what I considered acts of perseverance in fact left me with little to persevere for.

When reporters ask, I say with a smile, Yes, I still work as a model. And why wouldn't I? It pays well. The industry is full of friends. The reporters point out flaws, using some of the light criticism that was in my talk, and I say: But isn't that true for all industries?

If you read about Oldoini's work, again and again questions are raised about what she meant, whether she was feminist, whether she was an artist, how much agency she had. Critics and curators are often preoccupied with whether Oldoini was engaging in "collusion in her own objectification."[3] Challenging the either/or nature of whether she consented or refused, was complicit or naïve, is a key to understanding modeling. Instead, in the multiple portraits where Oldoini looks at the camera through a mirror, she offers us a more accurate way to understand her relationship to her own image: that it is not her own reflection that draws her gaze, but us, the audience, looking back at her, that she is so interested in. She lets us know she is aware of our looking, and that we are in a conversation.

The story goes that as Oldoini ages she draws her curtains, banishes mirrors, and rarely makes a public appearance. Yet at the end of her life she continues to visit the photo studio. Reading about Oldoini now, I am struck by a sort of lazy repetition as writers struggle to explain her later work. The general story arc goes: She comes to Paris as "the most beautiful woman in the world," then, as she builds a body of photographs and continues to make dramatic entrances in Parisian society, as well as diplomatic moves, she becomes "vain," her sense of self-importance inflated, and finally, as she ages and continues to place herself in front of camera, writers wonder, "Has she lost her mind?" Her project is now described as "strange."[4] They ask: "Did she know what she was doing?" I think these writers are confronted: If she is no longer a beautiful woman in front of the camera, then what is she possibly doing there?

3.

It's much better when you feel something from the photographer.
—NAOMI CAMPBELL, *Naomi*

Solomon-Godeau writes of Oldoini: "The lack of any clear boundary between self and image, the collapse of distinctions between interiority and specularity, are familiar, if extreme manifestations of the cultural construction of femininity."[5]

I think of the way a body can be simultaneously assaulted and aroused. Trying to make sense of this, researchers measured genital responses as they exposed participants to stories of consensual sexual encounters and then violent ones, and the results suggested to them that vaginal walls have evolved to lubricate in response to a wide variety of stimuli to reduce injury from unwanted penetration.[6] We evolve in reaction to the people and environments we find ourselves living in. "Lack of any clear boundary" is simply the human condition.

In the afternoon Hector photographs me in my underwear for a client. I am quiet and easygoing, but when I get home, all I want to do is sleep. *The New York Times* runs a story about my work. The same day, I can't figure how to change the dynamic on set where a photographer, who has worked less than two years, condescends and humiliates me repeatedly in front of a client I've had for a decade. He yells orders, comes on set to shove my body into the poses he wants, and mocks the poses I move into.

Because of the TED talk, press requests pile up, and I begin responding that I will only appear if I am joined by another person who rarely gets the limelight. A television producer replies by requesting headshots of the other feminist media makers who I insist join me on camera. On another network the host spends

95 percent of the interview focused on me, and the camera goes to a wide angle at the last minute to ask a single question of the organizer who joined me—a woman who could talk beyond fashion critique about her work building community with hundreds of young women and girls through a shared obsession with sneakers. I pull together a team and we start a small magazine with the intention of resourcing a rotating editor in chief.

As a model, I don't think I can get any more successful than I am right now. *Vogue, Elle,* and *Harper's Bazaar* covers, Prada, Tiffany, Calvin Klein, and Ralph Lauren campaigns, beauty and fragrance contracts, H&M, J.Crew, and Next, clients that shoot often and pay well, walking every runway from Chanel to Marc Jacobs to Victoria's Secret. This is as far as I can go. At least, if I cannot fully commit. This is as much access as I will have and as much money as I will make. I book every big job. If someone calls, Aimee answers and I get on the plane. But I make no effort. If they want more—if they want me to audition, if they want me to speak, if they want me to dress up, to commit more than two days, to attend multiple parties, to invent a product to sell—I cannot locate the motivation. I don't think about how to build a brand. I don't want more followers, I don't want to smile more, I don't want to lie more.

To build a career around my body required me to disassociate from the body. Like Oldoini, "like any great actress," as Nathalie Léger described her, we could only ever "pretend . . . to be pretending."[7] A performance that penetrated the skin was a prerequisite. And the ability to disassociate is also what made me successful: Without my own emotion getting in the way, the audience could find room for their own response.

The best intervention I can figure out next is to put other peo-

ple in front of the camera. I convince a large magazine to publish
portraits and profiles of some of the lead negotiators at the Paris
climate conference (the one that would go on to produce the first
legally binding global agreement). I jog alongside ███████ as she
walks between meetings at the conference. She hugs colleagues,
reminisces, makes them laugh, and ends with a jovial, diplomatic
send-off, looking forward, thank you, no thank you. As we walk
away she explains how someone we just spoke with undermined
negotiations to protect human life from climate catastrophe. I
ask her where she gets the energy. She tells me she keeps ginger
under her tongue. She tells me, or I ask her, about the lack, it
seems, of care in all this diplomacy. How do you deal? You learn
how to be like a man, she says with a laugh, and then offers:
Sometimes when the negotiations get heated or stuck at an im-
passe, she uses her allotted time to read a poem.

Humans coregulate. Our autonomic nervous systems inter-
act and constantly modify one another's behavior. In many relationships one partner (a parent, for example) may do the majority
of the behavioral regulating. I do not want to give up the tender-
ness that arises so easily from being agreeable. Capitalism's core
belief is that we ultimately act in our own self-interest. But how
does this explain the pleasure we get from serving others?

Back in the studio ████ moves my hair gently. Moves the strap
of the dress off my shoulder, puts it between my fingers. I have
seen her do this with other people she photographs: touch them
wordlessly, look into their eyes or at the light falling on their faces,
making them comfortable spending time together without speaking. The lighting is good and the hair and makeup are good and it
feels like she respects me. There is a good chance she does not, or
does not think much about me at all, but we have just completed

this big creative project together. I got the magazine to run it, organized the subjects, wrote the text, managed the social media campaign after it was published, and she took the photos and helped roll it out. We were both inspired by the work and the response.

I tilt my chin, open my lips, and look into the camera. I feel her looking back. I listen as she gives small adjustments, shoulder up, look back, that's it. I feel my nipples sharpen under silk in the wind from the fan. I slow under her gaze, the skin exposed down the sides of my chest expanding and contracting. We walk to wardrobe together and she watches me change. She asks me: Why don't you walk around naked all the time, with a body like that? I would if I were you. You are beautiful, I say. No, she says. I do not like that her celebration of my body seems to make her uncomfortable inside her own.

4.

It's only after reading multiple journals, books, curatorial statements, and magazine articles that I realize most authors are projecting their own confusion onto Oldoini and her photographs. Art historians Pierre Apraxine and Xavier Demange write that Oldoini "lived in a permanent state of rebellion, rebellion that *was without purpose, had no message,* but was fueled by her illusions."[8] Solomon-Godeau argues that Oldoini attempted to appropriate her "choreography of the self . . . for her own *ambiguous* ends."[9] But research reveals her ends were anything but ambiguous, her intentions being both nuanced and critical.[10]

The night before I shoot a big national ad, Aimee calls. They want you to write on cardboard signs something about protecting the environment. That sounds like greenwashing, I say. I know, she says, let me speak to them. She calls me back: They say you can write anything you want on the signs. But how, I ask, can a few words on a cardboard square be interpreted as anything else but activist? Tell them this will be a Kendall-Jenner-with-a-Pepsi-can type PR disaster. I can, she says, but they picked you, at least in part, for your activism.

I go for a walk. I have to keep activism and fashion separate, or bring activism to fashion in a way that genuinely raises our ambition and resists commodification. This could be an opportunity if I write all the things that this advertiser should get behind. All the things that should be normalized and run in a national ad on main streets across the United States. I can write "support the FABRIC Act," the federal legislation coming up for a vote that guarantees a minimum wage for garment workers, and "support the Fashion Act," the New York legislation that would bring more transparency to supply chains. I can say "end White supremacy," "expand the court," "asylum is a human right," "protect trans kids," "pay a living wage," "end the filibuster," "gun control now," and "divest from fossil fuel."

I text Aimee, "Okay, I have a plan."

The next day on set, blank cardboard signs are glued in a big grid to the wall, and someone passes me a black marker and a rolling ladder. I say to the art director, If we are going to write on protest signs, we have to say something real; we can't make a mockery of it. Well, what kind of thing are you thinking? he asks. I say, Stuff that the majority of our country supports, even if the majority of Washington doesn't, stuff like "abortion is healthcare." Okay, he says nodding. I walk to the set. The camera clicks. I start writing. I write as fast as I can before they can say cut. The set is quiet. When the ad comes out, the cardboard squares are blank. They look like nothing more than a textured geometric background.

Photographs are both limiting and expansive. On the one hand, what was inside my head is illegible, my words erased. On the other hand, centuries later Oldoini captivates viewers. People write about her, feel connected to her, project, as I am, their own thoughts and feelings onto her.

cheap, heavy earrings

1.

Like Grace Jones said: "I am diplomatic now. I could run for presidency now. I know how to play the game. But it's tricky for me to be diplomatic—it does not come easy. I find it manipulative and insincere. You have to manipulate your own self to get the results you need without actually expressing how you really feel."[1]

So when they ask me, Do I want to speak at the UN? Do I want to be a UN advocate for the Women & Trade Programme? I say yes, but privately I feel like this is an ugly affirmation that an Ivy League education and a couple *Vogue* covers really are as important as I feared. I need to believe that I can do good, and that I am better than the conditions that made my success possible.

Well, do I still want to be president? Mom asks when I call her to share my ambivalence.

Lincoln, Roosevelt, Roosevelt, Carter. Their names ring in my ears like nursery rhymes.

When I was old enough to ask about their flaws, I was told they were products of their time. The fact that FDR had been responsible for Japanese internment camps was acknowledged as unfortunate, but in school we learned mostly about the brilliance of the New Deal.

Now I learn the real architect of labor protections was Frances Perkins,[2] the first female cabinet secretary, and she was informed by organizers who embraced and educated her as a young woman (many of whom were young garment workers). I learn about Pauli Murray,[3] the lawyer, activist, and poet who was a longtime pen pal to Eleanor Roosevelt[4] and Thurgood Marshall, and who was, in 1941, the only student assigned female at birth in their[5] Howard Law School class. Murray's student paper provided the framework for the *Brown v. Board of Education* victory. Were they not also products of their time?

When they introduce me at the UN, it feels more than polite, it feels fictious. The list of compliments. The clapping. I think other people need to believe that I can do good too.

On the stage, in front of a couple hundred people, press, designers, diplomats, and the wife of the secretariat, I say: "I am so honored to be given the opportunity to be a conscious participant in an incredible supply chain, connecting directly to artisans whose work is deeply rooted in tradition and whose business supports thousands of women in developing economies."

I don't say: The fashion industry has a long way to go before it lifts women out of poverty. Jobs in this sector make up a large share of women's total employment, especially in developing economies, and these workers, of whom fifty million or more are women,[6] are rarely paid even half a living wage.[7] Certainly, this should disqualify the industry from being touted as a development tool.

Instead I say: "I have a deep respect for the incredible power of fashion to elevate the lives of women, to give them both an income and a voice, and I believe this program is a chance we have to serve a global community and sisterhood."

I worry that when I do not explain exactly where my income and my voice come from, I am helping export the American myth, the one that promises opportunity while it promotes hierarchy.[8]

I am probably just a celebrity stamp, and all of this is too self-absorbed. I'm just there to make sure *Vogue* writes up the show. I try to make myself useful and ask if I can send samples from the artisans to showrooms with which I have a relationship, but nobody replies to my emails.

2.

The hair dryer is going when I start reading about the factory collapse in Bangladesh. Over 1,000 people dead and 2,500 injured.

> Brigadier-General Siddiqul Alam, who is overseeing the recovery operation, said: "We have found a huge number of bodies in the stairwell and under the staircases. When the building started to collapse, workers thought they would be safe under the staircases."[9]

One thousand garment-factory workers producing clothes for companies I work for. Companies like the one we're shooting for today.

The first look is pleather pants, beige ankle booties, a gray, turquoise, and burnt orange sweater the styling notes call "Navajo,"* and cheap, metal earrings.

We are shooting outside in the sun against a white backdrop. I am sweating. I feel sick.

I go into the bathroom and have diarrhea. I don't want to go back out, and I stay in the stinky, sweaty, windowless room scrolling on my phone. I don't even get up and flush.

> Bangladesh has more than 5,000 garment factories, handling orders for nearly all of the world's top brands and retailers. It has become an export powerhouse largely by delivering lower costs, in part by having the lowest wages in the world for garment workers.[10]

I am being paid to be disposable, to sell clothes that are disposable, to sell something I have no right to sell, to be someone I dislike, to be uncomfortable, until I can no longer see my whole self because I also see what they see and give it willingly.

What higher value do I have? No other job would pay the day rate I'm making now.

The cheap, heavy earrings break when I take them out and leave my ears swollen and filled with pus.

---

* "Cultural appropriation in fashion has now gone seriously mainstream. [In one example,] the favorite read of tweens and teens everywhere, *Seventeen* magazine, featured this 'Navajo' fall fashion spread in their August issue. On many levels, I find this even more offensive than having a generic 'tribal fashion' spread. . . . They still rely on generalized Native stereotypes, but this time are referring to a *specific* culture. This points to the fact that in the collective American consciousness, all tribes are interchangeable." Adrienne K., "'Navajo' Fashion Spread in *Seventeen*," Native Appropriations, August 27, 2010, nativeappropriations.com/2010/08/navajo-fashion-spread-in-seventeen.html.

The industry does not depend on me alone, but I am part of it. All the clothes are too hot today.

An assistant has pinned photos of the looks we have to shoot onto a foam board, and I try to count them quickly before anyone notices. Eight by ten, but the last row is three short. Seventy-seven.

An EPA report finds a 1,000 percent increase since 1960 in clothing sent to landfills annually.[11] The numbers are so high it's hard to make sense of them. In 2018 nearly thirty-four billion pounds of textile waste ended up in the garbage in the United States. I divide by population: a hundred pounds per person. An average load of laundry is fifteen. That's nearly seven loads of laundry per person per year trashed. But this math distorts the responsibility. It ignores the billions spent advertising to drum up demand for these unnecessary products and the fact that brands overproduce, constantly discarding unsold garments as they introduce new trends weekly.[12]

It's just a job. It's just sitting, waiting, zoning out, and being a piece of a machine, and sometimes I'm too tired and it's too big and I'm just one piston.

But it is not a coincidence that the CEO of Zara was briefly the richest man in the world while his workers were some of the poorest. Nor that the head of LVMH is now the richest man in the world. In an industry where 97 percent of profits flow to just twenty conglomerates,[13] the primary motivation of the owners remains accumulation and consolidation of wealth. And they seek to advertise in whatever ways contribute to their goals and disguise their means: violent extraction that extends to both people (see, for example, the 2020 exposé that one fifth of the world's cotton was produced by enslaved labor[14]) and planet (see, for example, 2021 research[15] connecting one hundred of the largest brands to the deforestation of the Amazon through their leather supply chains).

My own career timeline almost exactly parallels and benefited from the explosion of fashion consumerism, a period (2000–2015) during which clothing production doubled.[16] While I made money, more and more garment workers became engaged in low wage and piece work, which means they were paid a few cents per finished garment and making a couple hundred garments a day still amounted to a less than livable wage. Even in the United States, at the time of writing this, there is no guarantee of a minimum wage for nearly a hundred thousand[17] garment workers.

I am not making enough conversation today. I work hard and fast, smiling, posing, skipping, silly. I overcompensate, winking at the crew, leaning my chin on the art director's shoulder, hugging the makeup artist, so we cannot hear my thoughts.

In representing a success accessible only to a very small group of young White women (and so few others that their exception proves the rule), my success reinforces that a racist hierarchy dictates who rises. And many poor women must be kept poor and invisible* for the industry to work as it currently does.[18] In countries where exports of ready-made garments make up the majority of export earnings (currently 84 percent in Bangladesh[19] and 70 percent in Cambodia[20]), the only local natural resource relevant to the production of those garments is women in poverty.[21] For this reason worker organizing has often been suppressed vio-

---

* "Tens of thousands of garment workers have forced a government riddled with corruption to take them seriously; yet they are invisible in the fashion media, because they're not legible to it. In skin color and class, Bangladeshi women garment workers don't look like the female powerhouses that are the revered subjects of fashion feature stories." Minh-Ha T. Pham, "Stories the Fashion Media Won't Tell," *The Nation,* January 18, 2019.

lently, and wages are kept low by both political and industrial leadership.

By elevating me for something I have no control over, the industry and economy signal to all women: There is almost nothing you can do or create that is as valuable as how you look. The better I am at being submissive, the better my chances of success. Even after working for so long, I am often made to feel I do not belong, that none of me is valued except what I cannot control— my youth, my race, my weight, my skin, my symmetry. I am a guest here, stopping by so long as age and trend allow.

Performance studies theorist Maurya Wickstrom argued brandscapes cause potential customers to experience a "somatic absorption . . . of the brand."[22] I consider whether modeling, the affective labor of sharing a brand's identity for the consumer to try on, requires the somatic absorption of late-stage racial capitalism.[23]

I think of Cindy Crawford's famous quote, "I see myself as a president of a company that owns a product, Cindy Crawford, that everybody wants. So I'm not powerless because I own that product."[24] And like her, the way Gisele was celebrated for commodifying herself: "Joe McKenna, a stylist behind some of the more influential fashion campaigns of recent decades, [said,] 'She always understood that "Gisele Bündchen" could be a business, too. And, though I loathe the word branding, that's exactly what she's always been aware of.' "[25] The way Naomi Campbell wrote, "We're a commodity to ourselves."[26]

A friend suggests I talk to someone, and so I make an appointment with a therapist. She says, Do you ever think about why your mom wasn't there?

No. (She doesn't ask about Dad.)

Why not?

Well, she had other kids, she had work, she had her own life, and I was an adult. I stop myself. The worst part of telling anyone these stories would be for them to blame Mom, or for Mom to blame herself. It was the sexist response, to find the woman to blame, despite all her efforts, even though she was not present or privy to the events and the adults whose actions were careless (mine included) were supported and encouraged by systems that existed before any of us arrived.

She cannot see us. I feel lonelier.

In the elevator I decide I don't want to speak with this therapist again; instead I want to find an honest economist. I need them to tell me why I should keep going in a system that made me more money selling my body than my mom made building a company that transformed an industry. I need them to tell me what contribution means to a society whose main purpose is to make money. I am considered valuable, but what value am I adding? And somehow economists always forget about slavery, colonialism, imperialism, and patriarchy. As if capitalism has no parents.

Here's what I know: Every day they remind me that I'm easily replaceable, and sometimes while I'm earning many years' wage, sometimes in a single day, they make sure I know I'm still worthless to the people who are paying me. So I understand money is unrelated to value and entirely interchangeable with power.

3.

I book a big campaign in LA. I haven't seen these guys in a while. At lunch Benjamin and the stylist are saying, I just don't understand American elections. What even is the Electoral College? Since I know, and can explain quickly, I try.

They cut me off. I just don't get it, Benjamin says over my words. I start again. It makes no sense, the stylist says to him. I try again. Why can't they hear me? It's just the three of us at the table. Why are they asking a question if they don't want an answer? They don't make eye contact. I swallow the answer and it feels like an ice cube, hard and stuck in my throat. It gives me a stomachache. Before they stand up, they look at me and say, You look so beautiful now, Camarones. You are not a little girl anymore. I don't say anything else.

In the fall Trump loses the popular vote and wins the Electoral College. Because for many years I have been informally organizing fashion models to attend marches and protests, getting activists and leaders in front of the camera and into mainstream publications, experimenting with what visible bodies might be able to perform and what our industry might do in service of movements, people are reaching out to me, distressed at the election results. I call Áine Campbell, a model who invited me to speak at one of the events she organized called "Beyond the Runway," a lecture series for models about how to build careers in and beyond fashion. We both know there is so much hunger for community, for education, for building power and doing something with modeling. In a few hours we have started a Listserv and planned a community gathering; a couple weeks later the "Model Mafia" has hundreds of members.

A job confirms and I check my boxes. What do I wear, how does my body look, how about my hair, take a shower, shave my legs, put some leave-in conditioner in, go shopping for a new dress, pack four pairs of shoes, relax forehead, should I try not to eat until the show or drink wine on the plane, whatever, I'm skinny, and they confirmed me, then again, this client likes to cancel girls backstage. I am disgusted to feel any of this, but then why am I going? Because it's a prestigious job and because back when I started, I sat on the floor for ten hours waiting to be seen by them for a casting and then let them bleach my eyebrows just to see how it looked. And now Aimee says: It will be easy, they really want you.

The airline is fancy. Business class is on the second floor; every seat has its own minibar, flat bed, dividers. Is this worth anything? To feel important, to feel that I'm going someplace, to feel that strangers value me.

In the immigration line at Malpensa, I see three models, a hairdresser, and an editor I know. We wave. There are two more models waiting at baggage claim. In the chauffeur line I see drivers holding signs with at least a dozen other names I recognize. There are two airline strikes and a taxi strike today. Everyone is saying they picked this moment because of Fashion Week. We are the people they are trying to wake up.

I had researched the history of labor organizing in fashion ahead of the first Model Mafia meeting. Before opening the floor I told the story of how one of the first labor unions in the United States was organized by the Lowell mill girls, young women garment workers. I share having learned that most of the labor protections we enjoy today were born out of garment workers organizing in the wake of the Triangle Shirtwaist fire. I remind us that some of the most powerful labor organizing was happening right now, at the other end of the fashion supply chain.

Àine and I made it a point to invite anyone who self-identified as a model, and to hear from models with a range of experiences, because even among models modeling is obscured: The fact that most models were young, immigrant women, far from family, making less than a livable wage, with tenuous housing, more than likely to experience assault and abuse and fall into debt, was largely unacknowledged. Instead the idea that models were rich and famous meant that many models considered themselves "aspiring," not "real" yet. Models, it turned out, were no exception in an industry largely made up of young women who are rarely in charge but do the bulk of the labor, the consumption, the culture making, and yet are treated as entirely replaceable. And when there were hundreds of us in the same room we could begin to see, feel, and dream of solidarity.

Yet when I get off the plane in Malpensa to work, I was crossing a picket line. How often did I do this without realizing it? Organizing by garment workers is barely even legible in fashion media. Fifty thousand garment workers strike in Bangladesh and not a single fashion outlet reports on the story.[27]

The hotel room is a suite. Walk-in closet, enormous bathroom, living room, bedroom. A plate of chocolate mousse with berries and chocolate writing that says my name and "Get ready to runway." The woman who brings me to the room says everything in the minibar is included, then hands me a free phone for the week. They don't do this for most of the girls. Many are waiting right now at the casting, going into debt to be here during Fashion Week. Upgrading their data plans so they can text their moms and search for directions to castings. And meanwhile they've put me in a seven-hundred-dollar-a-night hotel to do the same thing the other girls will do, walk stony-faced and square-shouldered down a runway.

I have to be at the atelier at 4:30 P.M. for Polaroids. Aimee calls to tell me not to mess them up. Okay. I shower. I put some makeup on, a little cover-up, a little brow, lip balm. Not too much. Important to look natural. I put on black jeans and a loose sweater. One hour until the driver comes. I sit down and stand up. I look out the window and change the thermostat in my room. I plug in my laptop, but I can't write. My head is empty. I tuck the sweater in at the front of my jeans and put on my new denim coat, purchased for just this occasion, and my new heels. I look confident and rich. I clearly own everything I'm wearing. I braid my hair. Simple, conservative. I'm not trying to be too glamorous or sexy; they know I can go there. I remind them with a little makeup and heels but keep it easy so I can fit whatever their image is—androgynous, youthful, womanly, whatever. I try on a couple other outfits but end up back in the first one. Finally the car is downstairs to take me.

The appointment is fast. Digitals in front of a backdrop, then some small talk and I can go. I cut two dozen girls waiting outside. Little girls with almost nothing except Whiteness for sale. In miniskirts and skinny jeans, cold, standing in lines or sitting on the dirty floor. I remember being one, watching someone more recognizable cut the line.

In the car back to the hotel I get a text from Aimee—a laughing emoji and a screenshot of her conversation with the casting agent asking how it went: the casting agent's reply, "omg, what has happened to cameron????" and Aimee's anxious "what? I just video chatted with her. What is going on?" And then the casting agent says, "just joking," and that I'm as gorgeous as ever. I reply "lol" but the exchange actually reminds me how precarious my position is. How my value, appraised by others, can go up and down on a whim.

redacted

At the time, I was totally unaware of ██████'s reputation. What I know now is a different story. There are a pile of articles, books, and stories you can easily find about his deplorable behavior, including accusations of rape. But I didn't know any of that then.

—JILL DODD, *The Currency of Love*

1.

Time passes quickly. Years pass and nothing happens. It is lonely. It's not just no language. Even our bodies can't speak; they are only used for what they can sell.

What if I tell you this: Even now, when I imagine us meeting to talk (if it was just us, and nobody else knew), I always imagine myself naked. I would have exercised for weeks just knowing the meeting was coming. I'd shower and condition my hair. Lotion from head to toe. Put on a little concealer, a gentle application of a shiny stick on the Cupid's bow and the lids and corners of the eyes, a lick of waterproof mascara on the lashes. You come to me. I'm waiting in some Frank Lloyd Wright–style country house, in late

August near a beach, maybe on stilts above a marsh, or on a dead-end road. Maybe I'd wear a worn cashmere sweater and bikini bottoms, relaxed, to answer the door. We'd both know there was nothing underneath. The sun would already be low in the sky and I'd offer you a drink. Whiskey? Music would be on, but I'd want your playlist. For the same reason I'm naked. I want you to be at ease. I want you to fall in love with me, and then I want to speak.

2.

In 1995 supermodel Veronica Webb told Rebecca Walker, for an interview entitled "How Does a Supermodel Do Feminism?," "I also think that if you are a woman, any way that you can amass power and money you have to do it as long as it's ethical, because it's just something that we don't have. And you know, it's funny, because . . . people say well, women trading off their looks strips them of their power, but it has empowered a lot of women. If you look at me, Cindy Crawford, Claudia Schiffer, Naomi Campbell, Elle McPherson, and many others, we've become phenomenally empowered by trading off our looks . . . "[1]

If money is empowering, if power can be amassed, and if they are worth getting "any way that you can," then it is also important to note who controls almost all the access, and what it takes to become a certain type of powerful.

A client wants me to shoot a trial so they can decide if they like me. If they like me, they'll confirm a one-year, 950,000-euro contract, which is the most anyone has ever offered to pay me.

Although we have never met or spoken, because you are the president of my French agency, you lead the negotiation.

When the job first comes up, I am almost certain that large sums of money are not empowering, but I am not so certain that I don't take the offer seriously. A million dollars is a lot. The amount of money required to bribe politicians to do horrible things isn't even that much. In 2015 *The Washington Post* reported that private prisons had "managed to quickly build influence" through funneling more than $10 million to candidates since 1989.[2] That's $10 million over twenty-six years, or just $384,000 a year.

I agree to the two-day trial.

After the shoot I think everything that happened on set was probably sexual harassment. When I tell Aimee she says, Your French agent is leading the negotiation, he's the one you need to talk to. But then, before I have the chance to call you, the contract gets signed. Aimee calls me back to tell me I got the job and suggests I send you flowers and a thank-you note. In the end it was all worth it, she says. I agree, it was worth it. I send you a card and flowers.

The following afternoon the contract is off. Aimee calls with the news and I say, Isn't that impossible? All parties signed. They only signed a deal memo, she says, not a contract. Maybe there could be a penalty for pulling out, she will see what she can do. But what happened? I ask. This all seems unusually chaotic. I didn't want to tell you, she says, but apparently the CEO of the parent company looked at the test photos and said you were too vulgar.

I was too vulgar? Did he see the images we took before they started making me do all those ridiculous things? What did you say? Did you tell them what happened? I tried, she says, but it would be better if you called your French agent directly. The CEO is his old friend. If anyone can say anything to change the situation it will be him.

I am so angry with myself. Perhaps it is because of how much money is involved; it is clear that I have a price. Or because at this point, I should know better. If you don't have money, that is a problem, but having lots of money, that's not a solution. Money, at best, is just harm reduction.

Before I called you I should have made a list of evidence. Instead I stumble through the story by using hours of the day as some type of narrative structure. I want to explain what transpired, but instead I tell you, because we both know it is true, that the plane landed at 11:00 A.M. and I got to set by noon.

I tell you the first half of the first day went well. Everyone was vibing and the photos looked good. At 5:00 P.M. they wanted me in fur. I don't wear fur, I said. But, they said, this is a test. The photos will never be published. I conceded.

At 6:00 P.M. the president came. She sat right in front of the computer. A request from her arrived to us on set, fifteen feet away, via an assistant: Change my hair.

We were never introduced, I don't know her name, there was no nice-to-meet-you. Instead she marched toward me while I was under the blow dryer executing her first request and said, with her eyes widening, Stronger, be stronger! Like this! and then she mimed pulling on an invisible necklace. She was annoyed, squinted at me, and seemed to want to escalate a drama whose origin was unclear. I nodded, half smiled, and told her: Okay!

She walked away and the art director, Jacques, came over. I'd only known him for six additional hours, but suddenly he was winking at me as if we were in cahoots and the president was an irritating stranger crashing our party. You have to be stronger, he said. She wants you to pull the necklace like it means nothing. Ten million dollars, it's trash to you! Okay? Okay, I said, I can try that. Good girl, he said.

We shot photos where I was pulling the necklace. When we paused, I walked over to the monitor to look. Come closer, the president called when she saw me craning. I bent down and she pointed at the image. Be stronger, she said thrusting her fist. The picture looked bad, the pose was ridiculous.

I got into another look. A ring with a gumball-size gem, a heavy collar necklace, and a strapless dress. Jacques, who also runs a misogynist porn magazine (which, in the past, he'd requested I shoot for, and I've declined) and is married to a woman I know, came up behind me and adjusted the weighty chain hanging down my bare back. I could tell it wasn't the stylist because there was too much gentle brushing of skin and too little movement of the necklace. I turned around and he looked at me. Bite the ring, he said, putting his meaty finger between his big, stained teeth. I could smell his breath. I bit the ring.

At 8:00 P.M. Jacques announced: Time for the naked shot. Then he walked over to me. Are you nervous? he asked, making eye contact for the first time in an hour.

No, I said, and anyway, I'll be wearing a bra. (He knew I wouldn't shoot nudes. There was a clause in the contract they signed before I came: no nudity.)

Well, he said, we'll see if that works. I need you nude.

The stylist's assistant helped me double-stick-tape a bra to my skin so that it stayed up without straps and gave me black underwear to put over my thong. I texted Aimee: "They are pushing for nudes and fur." She wrote: "I know the vibe is weird, but try to stay open, connected and collaborative with them and turn it around. Let me know if you want me to call the producer."

We started shooting and our set, which was a restaurant, started seating people for dinner and drinks, and they were staring. After we shot a couple rounds, the makeup artist asked me if

I'd like a foam wall put up for privacy and I said yes. A photo assistant pulled out a small piece of foam core that blocked nothing. Customers continued to stare.

Jacques sat down next to me on the couch and leaned back. I was in my underwear. A spotlight was hot on our skin. The crew and the restaurant were watching. He asked when I was leaving. Day after tomorrow, I said, and crossed my arms over the bra taped to my chest and leaned forward over my bare legs, pretending to stretch or be cold.

I'm leaving tomorrow night to Paris, for the ███ party, he said. You should come. The photographer had started shooting, so I didn't reply.

Okay, okay, I'll let you work. He stood up and walked off set.

The pictures from the second half of the day looked terrible.

At midnight, when I got back to my hotel room, I was mad because I didn't have the words to articulate clearly what Jacques was doing. I wanted to text Aimee. But what would I say? He walked away, refused conversation until it was on his terms? He engaged when I was less dressed? And this was my big contract he was putting at risk.

The next morning the president was pushier and had worse ideas. Lie on this fur, she said, now wink, now sexy, be like a snake, strong, strong eyes. Stand up, serpent, stand up. Be tough, be sexy, now laugh, throw your arms up.

I stood up and stepped over the fur. If I throw my arms up, I said, the coat will open. (My contract said no topless. And anyway, the idea of a topless ad for this client is ridiculous. Their ads run on billboards and in airports and magazines where laws prohibit nudity.)

Try it, try it, throw your arms up, be wild. She spent effort sounding exhausted, rolling her eyes, sending air out her nostrils like an angry horse, as if I was too uptight and difficult and she had to work extremely hard to get a good shot.

In front of a dozen people on set I threw my arms up and demonstrated that the coat opened, revealing my bare chest.

The photographer clicked.

It doesn't work, I said, putting my arms down. I looked at the photo assistant and she cropped the shot on the computer so it was just my face.

We took a break.

Jacques had changed his flight and was leaving the job midday. He came over to where I was standing alone in a patch of sun in the corner of the room to get warm between shots because we were now shooting outside, and said, I want you for my magazine, but whenever I request you they say you don't shoot nude.

I didn't say anything.

Do you shoot lingerie?

Yes, I said. (Best to continue to appear open and collaborative.)

Great. I have a lingerie campaign for you. Four days.

Nice, I said, that will be fun.

He told me he didn't know if I knew, but he was separated from his wife.

I'm sorry to hear that, I said. He looked at me and didn't say anything. He was waiting for me to react, to give him something. Nice working with you, I said. I gave him a hug.

In any other situation I would have told him to speak to my agent, which is code for "No the fuck way." I would have refused to wear fur, and to appear to be nude. I would have tried to say something pithy and direct to the president. I would have showed the art director I could care less about his approval by refusing eye contact and then speaking animatedly with the rest of the crew.

I think about how other girls manage. Maybe they are flirtatious with everyone, so there's no special treatment for the art director who demands it? A close friend reads this and tells me, You are being relentlessly self-punishing. Maybe. Maybe anyone who has experienced the expectation of flirtation would agree. Maybe if you have only ever flirted by choice you won't understand.

How is it that after so many years I'm still letting anyone tell me I must prove how willing I am by showing the crew my tits? How is it I join the art director in his disgusting fantasy and suppress my confident resourceful self for a self that is barely a self, that barely speaks, that nods, that is genuinely embarrassed to be caught up, but not for the reasons he believes? Of everything, pleasing him is what will make me win. And of everything, pleasing him is what will slowly erode any version of a self I have outside this moment. When I let his hand slide across my skin, when I arch my back and bite my finger for him, I am creating physical, material, accountable decisions. These moments exist.

But it's not just invisible labor to my clients, it's invisible to myself.* It is inside the seconds of contact between us where I understand his hand against me as power, and feel a dangerous electric thrill. To tell a good lie you have to believe it might be true.

In his withholding of attention and approval, he makes me want to please him, to prove, I can do that too, I am tough enough.

---

* "Managing themselves as 'ornamental objects,'" writes Mears, ". . . is seen as part of what models—and women generally—are, and not something that models do (West and Zimmerman, 1987, 141). The better a model's performance, the more invisible her efforts." Ashley Mears, "Discipline of the Catwalk: Gender, Power and Uncertainty in Fashion Modeling," *Ethnography* 9, no. 4 (2008): 431.

I hear you typing and guess you've put the phone down by now. Why do I have to convince you of anything? I do not want to take anyone to court. I do not particularly care if they pay me damages or face consequences. It's the fact that when I tell you, everything that happened is only allegedly, and I hear your skepticism because you never agree, you just stay quiet. I hear you ignoring me. My voice rises and all you hear is exaggeration, sensitivity, naïveté. What do you want me to do? you say. I guess nothing. I can't think of anything.

Aimee suggests I call you again and try to explain again. Better yet, she says, why not meet when you're in Paris next month.

I am telling you a story where we can't say why we did some things, where narrative details don't always provide meaning. Like when we think of Anita Hill we think of a Coke can, despite the fact that Coca-Cola really has nothing to do with it. Coca-Cola is part of an effort to put words, to make concrete, for those who cannot imagine. It's why when we think of Monica Lewinsky we all know the semen-stained dress was blue. Objects and outfits are more tangible, more believable, than we are. Evidence more important than shared meaning.*

---

* "The truth is that our gut-wrenching stories have been packaged and commodified for patriarchal consumption: tragicomedies that strip-mine our worst experiences for 'content,' whether on cable news or on your favorite feminist-lite website, which define us exclusively by that victimization. At no point is our expertise on our experience, or our analysis, really central. What people want are the gory details. It is, perversely, quite a happy fit for patriarchal norms about women in particular that we be seen as individuated damsels who are only good at being hurt and then singing about it." Katherine Cross, "Listening Will Never Be Enough," in *Believe Me,* eds. Jessica Valenti and Jaclyn Friedman (New York: Seal Press, 2022), p. 36.

3.

████████ messages me. All the sexual harassment allegations about Harvey Weinstein got her thinking: Why can't we call out harassment in fashion? She texts me about an early experience of sexual violence at work. What if I post your story anonymously?* I ask her. The whole industry looks at Instagram every day. I could remove the names and ask others to share their experiences. We know there are thousands of stories. We've been organizing. And even if nobody else wants to speak up, at least it will be a start. She agrees.

Within twelve hours my inbox is full. I cannot edit and post fast enough.

One model sends the account of the photographer she is accusing. I scroll through. She still likes his photos.

Speechlessness that can sound like consent tastes of nothing. It's easy to forget it's in your mouth.

Within forty-eight hours hundreds of people have messaged me. I keep posting. People are calling and emailing and texting. They are sending me stories they don't want public but want to share with me. Rape stories. Assault. Confusing stories with too many details to follow, screenshots of text messages and email evidence. Hundreds of people are commenting. Every person in fashion is reading this right now, Aimee calls and tells me. I post eighty stories. I take a break. Months ago the agency gave me a gift certificate to a hotel in upstate New York, so midweek my

---

* In 2014 Christine Fox used Twitter to collect and then share anonymous stories of what people were wearing when they were sexually assaulted to combat the notion that clothing choices were in any way responsible. It was powerful, and stuck with me for years, providing inspiration to carry out a similar style effort in 2017 with the belief that could help shift the culture of the fashion industry. Learn more here: https://www.theroot.com/what-i-wore-when-sexually-assaulted-women-of-twitter-1790885309.

partner and I go. My phone doesn't get service. My partner keeps asking me if I am okay. We are walking through the woods along a marsh. I am a comfortable five months pregnant. We adore each other. I am wonderful, I say.

At the hotel wifi works and people are still messaging me. More stories. And more messages telling me to take care of myself. I feel okay. I can see how grotesque and public this all is—alcohol/suck my dick/rubbing/a powerful photographer/I wanted him to like me/I was 14/he asked me if I was a virgin/he was a famous stylist/he kissed me/he pinned me down/I didn't say anything/I stayed and tried to think about other things while he raped me—but there is also a feeling of relief. It is painful and pleasurable to peel back, to expose, to flick a scab away and leave something raw, wet, open. Screenshots of emails from agents saying to suck it up. The language, the explanations, the manipulation, a repetitive, dull type of pain. I am only surprised that some of the people who are being named, whose names I am then removing—using my finger on the screen to draw a black line over the letters—are also liking the posts, commenting that this is unacceptable/powerful/keep going.

I start sending posts to other models and people in fashion to share. I send screenshots to seventy people.

I hear that people are talking on set and to their agents and clients. Texting their friends. We eventually will organize ourselves into a meeting of a hundred or so models and think about how to improve the situation. Nobody is sure what exactly is next: Buddy system? Training for agencies?

Press requests flood in. I ignore them. I do not want or need to distract from the chorus, to make it seem, as the media may want to tell it, that I am somehow the architect behind this outpouring, that it was not inevitable. Democratic storytelling works its own magic to make culture change. The stories are a type of negotiation; the more people who contribute, who share, who like, who comment, the more agreement forms around new norms.

The press want more eyeballs; they want a model to talk about anything related to sex and power. They want a model victim. They want names, scapegoats. And I do not want to reinforce the narrative of the victimized White woman in need of protection, especially because this often results in the expansion of the carceral state,* which by all measures I know does little to challenge the culture of violence that makes assault so common and acceptable in the first place.

I hear a ▆▆▆▆▆▆ reporter doesn't want to tell the story because: Weren't models just doing their jobs when these things happened? Weren't all people?

I can hear the cable news reporter: These girls you spoke with were raped and assaulted as young as . . . ? And I'd have to say: fourteen. The grotesque television lighting and makeup. Then they'd say, And has it ever happened to you? And I'd crumple and try to talk my way around it. Not because I felt secretive. But because what would be gained? Simply another story to reinforce this world order, to thrill audiences, to draw eyeballs to a network that wanted, more than anything else, to make money. Speaking to them would make it seem that the power to break a story still belonged to the same handful of legacy media gatekeepers.

Many people do not feel the same; they want to go to the press. I understand. My calculation is just one fallible opinion. So I connect those who want to speak with *The Boston Globe*'s spot-

---

* government systems that use punishment and control as the primary intervention, e.g., more policing, criminal laws, prisons, foster system

light team, who led the investigation that exposed rampant child
sex abuse inside the Catholic church. They have the resources and
experience to pull off an investigation of systemic abuse. The
Globe reporters say they will take their time, take months, and
interview hundreds of people. That seems powerful. Nobody
will have to stand alone, and the industry will be forced to acknowledge widespread abuse by every major player, all of us ac-
complices.

We go upstate again to walk in the woods, this time just for a
day. A model emails me and says she has a story about Finn. My
leg starts itching. I pull two ticks off the outside of my pants.

She was drinking. Finn had sex with her. She didn't want to.
She was younger than me. More intoxicated, perhaps. Maybe she
resisted more. She says she thought it was her fault. She says for
years they continued to be friendly.

When we get home there is a rash on both my legs and the
backs of my arms. I send a picture to my aunt, a midwife, who
says it's probably a pregnancy rash. It's so itchy. I have agreed to
speak at Glamour Women of the Year. I wake up at 4:00 A.M.
scratching and write a draft.

When I speak I want to explain what the press will never publish because there isn't hard evidence or, maybe, because there is
too much evidence. I want to explain how this type of abuse is
just the tip of the iceberg, how acquiescing to these gatekeepers
isn't a matter of consent when they are everywhere. When they
run the whole economy. Even Harvey Weinstein was tolerated by
movie stars and presidents alike: I find pictures of Hillary and
Barack with their arms around him, smiling. I want to talk about
how choosing not to consent is really only made possible by seeing alternatives to the entire power structure.[3] To avoid abusive
power means deciding that the power of these men isn't some-

thing we want,[4] isn't something that can make our lives better, or more just, or more sustainable. And when I work for them, I am participating, exploiting those further down the ladder.

I write about how my success, the one I pursued, reinforces a racist hierarchy. Reinforces that a woman's worth is quite literally superficial at best. It's not the salacious story with alcohol and hotel rooms. It's part of that story. It's why, when my breasts were still sore from growing and a man stuck his fingers inside me, I was quiet. Because accessing their power, their money, seemed worth it. I thought if I played along I could become powerful enough to force change, and I hate that this might be what has happened. It's why now I have to speak, even if I'm not making complete sense.

What use is this polished story of abuse if it can't expand, can't hold complexity? "This concept, of having to earn the right to have pain acknowledged, is predicated on a need to enforce that one party is entirely righteous and without mistake, while the other is the Specter, the residual holder of all evil," argues Sarah Schulman in *Conflict Is Not Abuse*. "If conflicted people were expected and encouraged to produce complex understandings of their relationships, then people could be expected to negotiate, instead of having to justify their pain through inflated charges of victimization. And it is in the best interest of us all to try to consciously move to that place."[5]

Have White people/White women inherited disembodiment? Do we learn carelessness and disregard as we are raised to tolerate and participate in abuse toward others and ourselves? I think of all the familiar directives lobbed at girls: chill out, don't be so uptight, stop overreacting, don't you think you might be exaggerating, you're being too sensitive. Raised in this culture, abuse can look so mundane and familial it can be hard to even identify.

1. "When Mr. Weinstein tried to massage her [Gwyneth Paltrow] and invited her into the bedroom, she immediately left, she said, and remembers feeling stunned as she drove away. 'I thought you were my *Uncle* Harvey,' she recalled thinking, explaining that she had seen him as a mentor."[6]

2. "I didn't feel threatened," she [Uma Thurman] recalls. "I thought he [Harvey Weinstein] was being super idiosyncratic, like this was your kooky, eccentric *uncle*."[7]

3. Janice Dickinson describes her abusive partner, photographer Mike Reinhardt: "Like my *father*, Mike made me feel I would never amount to anything. He would put me down at every turn."[8] And later she introduces her next partner the same way, "Mick became my new *daddy*. He was away much of the time, just like the rat bastard. And he wasn't particularly nice to me when he was around, which definitely made me feel right at home."[9]

4. Carré Otis describes her then agent and rapist, Gérald Marie: "Even as young as I was, I could figure out how my relationship with Gérald mirrored my dynamic with my *dad*. I had kept the secret of my *father*'s drinking. Now I was keeping the secret of Gérald's and my cocaine use."[10]

The stories remind me of all the photographers who told me to call them "Uncle." And all the men whose defense was "I have a daughter," whose daughters must have been thinking exactly the same thing: "I had a daddy just like you."

I was still scratching. The bumps on my arms started to welt. The editor at *Glamour* suggests I take out the line about Weinstein and political donations—it's a distraction—and the paragraph about race. How do I back it up? Everyone will point out that I still work in this industry. Am I quitting? I delete the paragraphs five minutes before the deadline.

By the time I speak, the rash is up and down my legs and arms. During a break, I call the ob-gyn and send her pictures. She recommends Benadryl and tells me to come in the next day.

Then it's back onstage. I walk out next to Anita Hill. I keep my hands clasped under my belly, holding shut the slits that would reveal my legs covered in bumps. Hill has the same clear, collected, presence as she did on TV in that blue suit in 1991. Just saying what is obvious over and over. After our segment is done, I ask her where she gets the energy to keep having this conversation, and she says she's exhausted and takes vitamin D.

The doctor runs her fingers over the bumps covering my body and takes some blood. She makes an appointment for me to see a dermatologist. At my last visit I told her that the ultrasound specialist she had referred me to stuck his hand below my underpants without warning. That he didn't tell me what he was about to do or ask if he could. Today she takes time at the end of our visit to let me know she called and spoke to him about it. He was apologetic. He would do better.

Schulman's thesis is that "at many levels of human interaction there is the opportunity to conflate discomfort with threat, to mistake internal anxiety for exterior danger, and in turn to escalate rather than resolve."[11]

The tests all come back negative. The dermatologist says she doesn't know what it is but I can try using steroid cream.

I ask my partner, Do you think this rash is from stress? I don't feel stressed. He says, Maybe it's the body getting rid of something. He says, How could it not be connected?

I make an oatmeal bath and, for a minute, let myself scratch. I haven't touched the rash for three weeks, and now I let my nails go over and over the bumps as hard as they can. The release is almost orgasmic. My entire body and brain let go. I stop so I don't bleed. My legs burn in the milky water. The next day the rash is gone.

A friend tells me women don't remember giving birth very well. Memory is actually much worse when we're stressed, she says. A patient of hers sent flowers and shared the birth story she'd posted on her blog. I'd say 90 percent of what she wrote didn't happen, she says. So, she continues, we can't really trust what women say. What I'm saying is, just read with a grain of salt, or don't read too much.

4.

After I write, I shower.

In the shower I begin to list all the ways I may have told this story wrong. All the details I left out.

I didn't include the other time I visited Finn in a hotel room because I can't remember exactly what happened. Or the time I tried to tell another girl and she whispered, Who was it? and I lied and told her the wrong name, someone even more obvious, I thought. How awful is that? I told her not to tell anyone. I only wrote about a few people, treating a person like a parable. And I didn't say nearly enough about the people I love working with.

I flip through model memoirs. I browse Carré Otis's book again. "I disappeared,"[12] she writes after ▮▮▮▮ raped her.

That name. I know that name. I google him. Oh! It's you!

You! The head of my French agency. We've spoken on the phone about that stupid test shoot, the one I referred to in my head as: stuff I'd do for a million dollars. I have an email from you in my inbox. You were supposed to be negotiating on my behalf.

Aimee told me you wanted to have dinner. Talk to him, she said. Tell him what you're telling me. He's the one negotiating the whole thing.

You ended up canceling last minute. The photographer I was shooting with that day asked who I was texting. I tell him it's you, my agent, and he laughs and says you're an old friend. Well, I tease, Then tell your friend you can't believe he's standing me up! And so we call you together.

When you answered, the photographer shouted playfully, You're standing up this beautiful woman? You're a fool!

Then he passed me the phone.

I'm sorry, chérie. My flight was canceled. Next time.

Then there were flowers in my hotel room right next to my bed with a note from you apologizing. In your place another agent came to dinner, and when we finished eating I gave her the bouquet. I won't be able to enjoy them, I told her, I leave in the morning.

Now I find some relief that I did not sleep beside them.

I was angry then and I am angrier now. I was too vulgar? When I point out that I was coerced into those shots and that anyway, the contract was already signed, the shoot dates booked, you told Aimee I couldn't go up against ███. What would I do? Take a billionaire to court? This is why, you told Aimee to tell me, ink on paper doesn't mean anything.

I google you. An anonymous essay published by a former model dates public allegations going all the way back to the eighties. "The highest ranking female executives . . . quit after demanding that ██████████ and █████ . . . stop having sex, er, raping, underage girls."[13]

Then I find:

1. Ebba Karlsson, who modeled in the nineties, says you slipped your hand under her skirt and fingered her.[14]

2. Shawna Lee, a then-fourteen-year-old model from Canada, told *The Guardian* that instead of taking her home after partying at Le Bains in Paris, you brought her back to your apartment and pressured her to join you in bed. It was her first sexual experience.[15]

I leave the quiet library room where I am writing and call a friend, another model, from the staircase. Can you believe this? She says, Whoa, and then, But it's not anything we didn't already know, right? I watch the snow falling outside the window. It reminds me of home. Fast and bright, covering everything in white.

Last week I met with BRAC, a nonprofit supporting garment workers in Bangladesh. They told me how their university was mapping the garment factories and exactly which brands they produced for. How the data would be made public any day now. For how many decades had industry PR claimed traceability was impossible? And now, on a shoestring budget, university researchers were doing it. How easily the whole thing unravels once we start taking notes.

I text Aimee: "Did you know about ███████? That Carré Otis says he raped her? That they made a documentary, an exposé, and he suppressed it?" I send her the article:

3. "███████ was filmed on hidden camera by the BBC trying to give a 15-year-old model £300 for sex, and bragging of how many entrants to the Elite Model Look competition—average age 15—he was going to sleep with that year."[16]

She calls.

They're all part of that time, she says, drugs and, you know. I can make my own assumptions but I don't know what happened. I don't know if it's real or not. I've never really confronted him. He denies it. In my personal opinion he's one of those slimy French guys. Can you sit down and talk to him and he's going to be polite? Yeah. In all my interactions with him it's just work. That was decades ago. When we do talk on a personal level, he talks about his daughter and taking her to school and how they're going away to the countryside. But his history, yeah, it's hardcore. But it was during a hard-core time. But you know it's everywhere.█████. ███████. You know.

I know.

We hang up.

Why have prisons or criminals if we're all okay with the men at the top walking around raping people and running everything?*

---

* See Mariame Kaba and Eva Nagao, "What About the Rapists?," bit.ly/WhatAboutTheRapists .static/5ee39ec764dbd7179cf1243c/t/6109e65d5a8ce56464ff94eb/1628038750972/WATR+Zine .pdf.

4. Karen Mulder accused you of rape in 1992, and according to *Jezebel* you paid for her stay at Montsouris hospital following a suicide attempt.

5. And now I remember another model, Jill Dodd, mentioning your name. I find the scene in her book quickly. She writes that she screamed for you to stop but you continued fucking her until you came.[17]

I should quit; I should reread this list to remind myself to find other work. Not because of you, you were just a symptom of a profoundly broken industry. I tell Aimee I want to leave your agency. I can't speak publicly on this issue and be represented by him, I tell her. But, she says, the agency isn't his, it's actually owned by our New York agency. So fire him, then.

Yes, I told her to fire you. You have more than enough, and you will be fine. And how can you continue as the boss without so much as an apology?

Anyhow, they don't fire you. So I leave. It feels irrelevant.

The Guardian publishes an article[18] where even more women come forward alleging you raped them.

6. Wendy Walsh

7. Ann Maguire

8. EJ Moran

You still work in the industry, you still run the agency, but you take your LinkedIn page down.

"Could ██████ have thought that the friendship we had

forged, the fact that we did drugs together, the fact that I lived in his house, all indicated, in some way, that I was amenable to having sex with him that night?" Carré Otis asks in her memoir. "I can't say. I can only know that I never asked for it. As far as I'm concerned, the sex we had that night was not consensual."[19]

A *New York Times* report[20] adds

9. Assault allegations from Lisa Brinkworth

You "categorically deny" all accusations.[*]

5.

I looked at thousands of images of horror of different kinds from all over the world: famine, disease, epidemics, terror attacks, houses torn down, butchered bodies, bombings, torture, mass death, and poverty . . . until I noticed that one image was absent from the various sites—newspapers, photo albums, television programs—in which images of horror are shown: the image of rape.

—ARIELLA AZOULAY, *The Civil Contract of Photography*[21]

Visual culture theorist Ariella Azoulay asks: "Has anyone ever seen a photograph of rape?"[22]

---

[*] On Feb 13, 2023, a French court decided your "case was closed because of the statute of limitations." In response to the ruling your lawyer said, "With this decision, it is now established that ████████ is and will remain innocent." *The Guardian* article reporting on your trial concluded by mentioning that another French agent who was charged with rape and imprisoned in 2020 "like [Jeffrey] Epstein, . . . killed himself while in a Paris prison in February." How completely these penal systems fail at changing or challenging a culture of violence.

In the stories people sent to me of experiencing sexual assault in the fashion industry, many mentioned the presence of a camera and some included that they were penetrated, groped, massaged, mounted, etc. while a photographer was shooting. These images exist, and a good many must already be public, so I want to ask: *How many photos have we seen of rape?*

When Azoulay does not gain permission to share a photograph with the context she wants to provide, she traces it, and shares the tracing. Were we to identify the archive, it would reveal a formidable stunt. My performance was intact even on the day my voice disappeared, the photos entirely indistinguishable from thousands of other fashion photographs.

Scientists say suppressing the expression of an emotion can reduce the feeling itself.[23] In a study published in *The Journal of Pain,* subjects who were told not to frown experienced less pain than those who grimaced when heat was applied to their arm. However: "People who tend to do this regularly might start to see the world in a more negative light. When the face doesn't aid in expressing the emotion, the emotion seeks other channels to express itself through."[24]

After model Wallis Franken's suicide, her friend and fellow model Tracy Weed described her to *Vanity Fair:* "Wallis was a master of fitting in. We didn't learn any of the things that people who grew up more normally learned, like who you are, what you want, what is good for you and what is bad."[25]

When you spend time calibrating for the mood and comfort of those around you, it's like a radio that's always on. When it turns off, emptiness. What to do with the body when the rhythm is gone? Think about how everything looks. It looks too material. The table is imposing and solid, the room gets smaller, the light isn't right. What to think about inside all the silence?

In the middle of the night my phone rings. It's Emma. She tells me Irina killed herself. She asks if I know her mom's number. I don't. Or can I call her agent? I can, I whisper.

At Irina's small viewing (the funeral would happen later, back home) she lay in heavy makeup, her body clothed in a dramatic dark-maroon lace dress—high neck, long sleeves—that her mom had brought. She had jumped from her window, but she looked so put together under thick makeup. I don't remember anyone speaking. Instead we were invited to sit in rows of chairs organized to face the casket and a flat screen hanging above her, which cycled through a slideshow of modeling pictures. There she is in her underwear. They kept the logos; they are showing all the ads.

I watch the slideshow five, six, seven times. When we leave, they give us a laminated card with her picture.

"You don't see rape, you don't see any woman being raped," Azoulay writes. "What you do see are lots of abandoned female bodies, susceptible to rape. . . . Disclosure of rape images to the gaze would reveal that there is nothing in them more terrible than in other images of women, which exhibit their sexual accessibility and make manifest their abandonment."[26] Women, she argues, in the realm of the visual, are still objects, still something to be possessed. Rape is just the logical conclusion, the way to ultimately possess someone/something. Is this why, after writing five hundred, six hundred pages of draft, my edit brings me back here?

In writing I allow myself to slip into the well of speechlessness and find that sinking is easiest. The sounds, even of my own voice, echoing and distorted above, make no sense.

Ayesha Barenblat, founder and CEO of Remake, an organization fighting for fair pay and climate justice in the fashion industry, gave one of the most succinct and clear statements of the industry's impact that I've ever read. The fashion industry, she told *Yes!* magazine, "is depleting and violent to women's bodies and the environment."[27]

When you are speechless, the last place a story lives is in the body. And the body keeps bringing me back here.

In her appeal for respectful working conditions, Edie Campbell described working as a model: "When models go on set, we enter into an unspoken contract. For that day, we surrender our bodies and our faces to the photographer, stylist, hairdresser and makeup artist. . . . The power imbalance is huge, and the duty of care to that model is even greater as a result."[28] Under what circumstances can one consent to their own objectification? Can a fashion image ever be of a woman who isn't an object? Can our objectification ever do anything but undermine our humanity? Certainly there are instances of giving over our bodies that are pleasurable.

Azoulay finds a photograph she argues is "far more important for understanding the phenomenon of rape during the period in question than the photograph of a certain crime scene might be, where say the specific rape of a particular woman actually took place . . . [because it] contains lessons for us concerning the general conditions created by the emergency military government for the abandonment and rape of Palestinian women."[29]

What photograph could there be of the conditions that make violence inside the fashion industry possible?

An editorial published with the title "Pretty Wasted" shows models in short, sexy party dresses, high heels, and ripped stockings laid passed out on the floor, splayed across folding chairs, slumped against concrete walls, surrounded by broken bottles, beer cans, spills, and grime. I almost shot the story but ended up not being cast (possibly because Aimee asked for the creative brief). A friend who was in some of these pictures tells me when they were published people on the internet were angry and left comments asking what were the models thinking, posing like that? She told me it was a night shoot in the middle of Fashion Week, she was tired, she was unhappy to be lying on the floor next to broken glass and wanted it over with. And anyway, what was she going to say, working with such an important photographer and stylist? I feel lucky to have avoided the negotiation.

The conditions that make violence such an acceptable fantasy that it gets published? A system that celebrates domination and makes it look aspirational.

a quilt-making theory

1.

The first time I try to finish this book Aimee calls. ███ was raped by ████████. He is the photographer of the moment and has just signed half a dozen major contracts with the biggest brands and magazines.

This is not how I wanted to end the story.

The second time I try to finish, I meet a woman who tells me that she used to model in the eighties. She pulls out her phone to show me the *Vogue* covers. How did you find the work? I ask. I was assaulted near the end of my career and it kind of ruined my twenties. That's terrible, I say. Was it ████████████████████? I don't know why I blurt out his name. Her face lets me know it was before she says yes. I'm sorry, I say. Sorry for naming him. It just came out. I'm—It's okay, she says. We talk about the exceptional weather before parting ways.

This is not my story. Perhaps it was where I started, when I wished to take my mom's place, to feel on her behalf. But now? Didn't I say, "I chose to be here"? And didn't I continue to choose, to try to walk some fine line where I could work and organize, have access and speak my mind? I couldn't figure out the math of walking away. I want to raise my ambition. Consent is too low a bar. It is the bare minimum. I want more choices for all of us, more life-affirming life-sustaining choices, jobs, relationships, and cultures.

I still feel humiliated when I am introduced as a model. I know sexism informs this feeling: The fact that this industry, and this job, celebrates young girls makes it a target for derision and disgust. And I know my value: How my experience of embodying a commodity, as well as finding ways to resist commodification, and working to use it in service of change, has equipped me with the ability to critique and help transform a culture of consumerism into one of care.

The main job of a model is to learn to predict what feeling your body will elicit in someone else's body. The easiest way to do this is to work within shared stories. It has been argued that there is a "half-second delay between image perception and cognition of its meaning . . . a space in time between when the image affects us and when we figure out what it means."[1] To make photos is to dwell in the half second before cognition. To know that we feel before we think.

The shared story of the fashion industry is that behind the curtain there are vulnerable women and powerful men, extractive business practiced by greedy corporations, and girls who know how to argue we're empowered by objectification. How do we change a story that is widely accepted?

William Shepherd wrote one of the most poetic and grotesque eyewitness accounts of the Triangle Shirtwaist fire, which
killed 146 garment workers, mostly young women, many of
whom jumped to their deaths to escape, whose bosses said they
had locked the doors of the factory to prevent theft.

> The first ten thud-deads shocked me. I looked up—saw
> that there were scores of girls at the windows. The flames
> from the floor below were beating in their faces. . . .
>
> I even watched one girl falling. Waving her arms, try-
> ing to keep her body upright until the very instant she
> struck the sidewalk, she was trying to balance herself.
> Then came the thud—then a silent, unmoving pile of
> clothing and twisted, broken limbs.
>
> As I reached the scene of the fire, a cloud of smoke
> hung over the building. . . . I looked up to the seventh
> floor. There was a living picture in each window—four
> screaming heads of girls waving their arms.[2]

This haunting two-dimensional "living picture" captures
these young women as perpetually helpless victims in the moments before their death.

Yet all of their names are known—starting with Lizzie
Adler, twenty-four, Anna Altman, sixteen, and Annina Ardito,
twenty-five; to multiple Bernsteins, Essie, nineteen, Jacob, thirty-
eight, Morris, nineteen; to young Ida Brodsky, fifteen; to Kate
Leone, fourteen; and all the way at the end of the alphabetized
necrology, Sonia Wisotsky, seventeen. Their stories are known
and the testimonies of their co-workers who survived are recorded. They had organized and gone on strike for better condi-

tions a year earlier, and in the wake of their deaths, worker protections were finally passed as part of the New Deal. Their work had been preceded by the organizing efforts of the teenage Lowell mill girls, who formed one of the first labor unions in the United States and who were also inextricably linked to enslaved Americans—as mill girl Lucy Larcom wrote, "When I've thought . . . what soil the cotton-plant we weave, is rooted in, what waters it—the blood of souls in bondage—I have felt that I was sinning . . . to stay and turn the accursed fibre into cloth."[3] And it is the centuries-long fight for freedom, by those enslaved, forced to work in cotton fields, and their descendants, that makes possible so many democratic rights we enjoy today. And all of this is no less true than the living-picture girls in peril, but somehow, that makes for easier poetry. I suspect because so much of our culture is organized around villains and victims, climaxes and perfect girls, and not the slow everyday work of making a livable world.

A friend emails me to ask if I can speak at their fashion activism lecture series and say something that focuses on "tangible ways people can be part of a solution, not just reiterating the same depressing facts." We cannot escape perpetuating the industry's violence if we do not find words for it. Then again, I feel I erase twenty years of who I have been by articulating that violence, so visceral it's hard to remember everything else: the way we organize; the way we can make beautiful images of a future worth pulling closer; the way fashion can be such a powerful collective form of expression; the way the people laboring inside this extractive industry also have a long history of making powerful change.

2.

When I started writing I watched Sinéad O'Connor's 1991 interview with Arsenio Hall at least forty times. In it she explains she has decided to boycott award shows because they promote "material success" and the idea that it will make people "happy." She says, "We as a race are concerned with material success rather than with each other, we don't love each other, we don't care about each other."[4]

I obsessed over unraveling how much of her was wise and how much was naïveté. How much of her stardom was connected to her beauty, her Whiteness, her youth, her femininity, her vulnerability, her agreeableness, and how much, if at all, she was consciously performing those things—the way she did her makeup, the way she smiled and averted her eyes, giggled, played with her shaved head, listened intently, allowed herself to be interrupted—and how much of all of that, on top of her incredible talent as a musician, was what made her powerful activism possible.

The interview is brilliantly unrehearsed and complex. At one point she critiques an American musician calling for peace in the Middle East—"I don't know what that means when you're dressed in a suit that's made out of the American flag"—and in response, Hall stands up and turns to show her and the audience the flag emblazoned across the back of his leather jacket. "Kind of like this?" She laughs. She looks for the language to explain it's okay to be proud of some parts of a thing, and also critical.

I watch it again. After all these years I am still riveted.

When Hall asks her about a DJ who suggested she be spanked like a bad child, and adds he'd like to do the spanking, she replies, "What are you doing later on?" in what looks to be genuine flirtation, or, just as likely, is a flawless performance. How familiar that feels. Perhaps, like me, she did not know (yet) if she was performing.

A friend reads this book and sends me a James Baldwin quote: "The price one pays for pursuing any profession or calling is an intimate knowledge of its ugly side."[5] I started working when I was sixteen and soon filled with righteous indignation at the way the fashion industry worked, and the way the whole world seemed to work. And the longer I worked, the harder it was to see myself as separate from the industry's failings. I'm not separate. But I am, we are, more than them.

I get older, and when I rewatch the video I am overcome with admiration and a desire to care for O'Connor—how young, tender, brave, and thoughtful she is. And I want to feel that same care and admiration for my younger self.

3.

I'm at Grandma's. I go outside into her yard and admire a three-foot-tall cactus she has painted with purple acrylic. From over the fence her neighbor jokes, If you stay too long at Ms. Shirley's house, you'll get painted too.

Almost nothing here is left untouched. Grandma has painted the trash cans. The toilet, "Because it was just so ugly," she says, glaring at the raised white plastic commode, now with painted pink tendrils and collage cutouts. She's painted the wood floor in her bedroom and entryway, the tiles outside in the carport, the front of the dishwasher, and every stair. Glancing up at the empty space on the ceiling of the kitchen, she muses, "I just don't know how I could reach it with my brush." Around the house there are news clippings picturing the women's fashion collective she started in Egypt and relics from the craft market she organized in Swaziland. In her closet there are decades of dresses she sewed that I try on and come out twirling for us, thrilled to find their zips and clasps pull the fabric just exactly over my shape as it had hers.

Grandma has altered nearly everything she wears, including swimsuits, sewing watches from garage sales onto the necklines because "I'd lose regular jewelry in the pool." Mom rolls her eyes, but I've watched her wind balls of yarn in her lap, cut thread with her teeth, and knit through meetings, car rides, television shows, and babysitting, making sweaters for us and for the neighbors and once even for some trees. When I was a kid, she made clothes to my exact specifications: a jumpsuit with balloon pants in blue gingham, vest top in ladybug, lined with red flannel.

Activist Mariame Kaba has written: "Let's begin our abolitionist journey not with the question 'What do we have now, and how can we make it better?' Instead, let's ask, 'What can we imagine for ourselves and the world?' "[6]

That women's creative practices have usually been dubbed "craft," our making for an audience that rarely extends beyond the home, an exclusion from capitalism and the hierarchical power of the art and fashion industries, gives us one road map for how to move beyond them, toward culture that sustains us.

Fred Moten wrote, "What if we could detach repair not only from restoration but also from the very idea of the original—not so that repair comes first but that it comes before. Then making and repair are inseparable, devoted to one another, suspended between and beside themselves."[7]

A quiltmaking theory of storytelling: Save and collect things, especially those worn beyond repair. Honor the labor that came before. Cut and piece together. Sew. Iron. Stand back. Cut, sew again. Allow for pattern and juxtaposition to provide narrative structure. Allow feeling to inform logic, use a quilter's math, sometimes intricate, sometimes improvisational, to dictate form.

I read through our old emails. Grandma had written me:

Three of my friends use ponds cream and they have gorgeous complexes [I assume she means complexions] and i am now using that. I met my Face Lift Doctor in the Betty Griffin house [the thrift store] and he now has a long Pony Tail and a simple very natural girlfriend that was with him. We had a great visit and i told him that my friends don't believe I am 92 so the two face lifts i had when i was sixty and eighty and paid five thousand dollars each [for] worked. I was the first one he ever gave a face lift [to]. Good luck on having your baby cam. We are all glued to the computer waiting for the message. LOVE

Whenever I call her, she reminds me she wanted to be remembered as an athlete first. It's all about the breath, she always says on the phone. She won gold, silver, and bronze medals swimming at the Senior Olympics. Framed all over her home are news clippings about the number of pull-ups she did at the local athletic club and about her training regimen, and profiles with pictures of her standing on podiums wearing long swim bathrobes and medals around her neck.

The things modeling taught me to be skeptical of—fame, material culture, ornamentation, being seen primarily as a body—she delights in.

When I am in labor with our youngest child, my partner takes the older two children out of the house to stay with my stepson's mother, and I am at home alone. I track contractions for a while, every two minutes, and somehow painless this time, so I stop and wonder how to be inside an afternoon with no demands, no work, no one else to please. I lie in bed. I tell myself to find by tracing, like a finger along skin, what is pleasurable. I am not sure why, but I decide to rifle through my sock drawer, our bathroom drawer, and finally the junk drawer until I find a small unopened hotel sewing kit. For no reason, other than that I am suddenly curious, I want to make a quilt.

My work is crude. I have no sewing machine and the only stitch I know is over-under-over-under. The stitches are neither straight nor regular. I barely have patience for knots; instead I make a few loops, cut, and keep going. Making a quilt compels me, and it must be true for those who love making clothes too, because it is an art we intend a person to use, to keep a body warm.

acknowledgments

I am grateful that Caroline Eisenmann reads her DMs. From our very first email exchange, she gave me the gift of seeing the most ambitious possibilities of my writing. Her steady confidence in this book made so much room for me to take risks on the page. Thanks go to her and the whole Francis Goldin Literary Agency for including me in their many decades long commitment to writing as activism.

Thank you, Marie Pantojan, for the easeful editing process, for letting me talk out ideas, and for responding to my last-minute marginalia. Thank you to everyone at Random House. To have a team thinking about how to make meaning from these experiences is the gift of a lifetime.

Thank you to Carrie Plitt for agenting this book in the UK, and editor Cecilia Stein, and the team at Oneworld, for being a bonus publisher I didn't even know was an option. I am grateful for your thoughtful feedback and support.

The Mesa Refuge residency invested in me as a writer before anyone else did, and provided a beautiful shed with the view of an estuary where I wrote the first two chapters. Manuel Pastor and Andrew Boyd, my co-residents there, were the first people who ever read pages and their warm reception gave me encouragement to keep going.

I am grateful to Janani Balasubramanian, a wonderful writing partner and friend, and for the dozens of shared focused work sessions followed by long walks and bike rides that made writing a joy, and never a lonely practice. And thank you, Lawrence Barriner II, for having the idea to do a stay-at-home writing retreat; the days we spent together supercharged this project.

Thanks to Hawa Arsala, Al Bland, Megan Eardley, Jaclyn Friedman, Landon Newton, Linnea Russell, and Christiana Tien Tran for reading drafts. Megan, more than once. The notes, conversations, and reading recommendations they shared were such powerful and unexpected expressions of love and care for which I am profoundly grateful. Thanks to Jess St. Louis and E. B. Bartels for reading chapters when I got stuck and offering generous feedback.

I am also indebted to Christiana Tien Tran for being a partner on every single fashion project I've worked on over the past fifteen years. Her willingness to explore what meaningful work we might make inside and alongside the fashion industry, no matter how fantastical, strange, or potentially difficult, has helped me continue to see opportunity and think with playful abandon.

To the people who reminded me that there is another narrative structure, where the completion of everyday tasks pulls the story along, thank you. Roy Russell (Dad) whose cooking/cleaning/

fixing taught me the deep fulfillment that can come from main-
taining the world right around us, and whose labor has always sus-
tained me in more ways than I can know, thank you. Mary Louise
Bedard, who nurtured our middle child while I wrote and edited a
lot of this book, thank you. At Mrs. Bedard's playgroup, daily,
weekly, and seasonal rituals contain purpose, growth, and joy. Both
of them helped me consider that the response to something broken isn't a big resolution, it's in the sweeping, baking, planting,
building, and caring for the world we need to live in every day.

Thank you, Anastasia Myslyk, for the hours of childcare, and
for your contagious determination. Thank you, Dylan Russell,
for all the uncling, and for taking our five-year-old on long, rigorous outdoor adventures. Thank you, Lawrence Barriner II, for
taking the baby often before I thought to ask. Thank you, Malvina
Baker, for the incredible gift of a stepson, and for loving up all our
kids.

Thank you, Damani Baker, for building a life with me that has
space for grief and pleasure, art and children, adventure and
peace. When we were just getting to know each other, I shared
my favorite essays and books by sending him voice recordings of
me reading sections out loud. In the evolution of that exchange,
I spoke most of this book to him before ever writing anything
down. In so many ways, he made it possible for me to write.

I am grateful for our magnificent children—Kohli, Asa, and
Shola. Being their parent is the most serious and wonderful responsibility, and guides and grounds me to approach all moments
with as much intention and hope.

Robin Chase (Mom), thank you for reading drafts, caring for
children, and most of all for sharing your life with me, and for
letting me share this small part of our story. I love you.

notes

does the baby have dimples?

1. Susan Sontag, *On Photography* (New York: Farrar, Straus and Giroux, 1977), p. 4.

you're a gemini

1. Kirstin Downey, *The Woman Behind the New Deal: The Life of Frances Perkins, FDR's Secretary of Labor and His Moral Conscience* (New York: Knopf Doubleday, 2009), p. 69.

2. Cassius Dio, *Roman History, Volume IV: Books 41–45,* translated by Earnest Cary and Herbert B. Foster, Loeb Classical Library 66 (Cambridge, Mass: Harvard University Press, 1916), p. 169.

3. Frances Perkins, labor secretary for FDR and the first female cabinet member in the United States, "learned . . . that the way men were able to accept women in politics was to associate them with motherhood. 'They know and respect their mothers—ninety-nine percent of them do,' she explained. She began to see that her gender, a liabil-

ity in many ways, could actually be an asset. To accentuate this opportunity to gain influence, she began to dress and comport herself in a way that reminded men of their mothers. . . . She even kept notes on her exchanges with men. . . . She called these observations 'Notes on the Male Mind.' The transition to the somber black dress, the pearls, the matronly demeanor were subtly picked up in the press reports. Before . . . the media had characterized her as perky, pretty, or even dimpled. . . . Now she looked and dressed like a sedate middle-aged mother." Downey, *Woman Behind*, p. 69.

4. Elizabeth Winder, *Marilyn in Manhattan: Her Year of Joy* (New York: Flatiron Books, 2017), p. 37.

5. Irin Carmon and Shana Knizhnik, *Notorious RBG: The Life and Times of Ruth Bader Ginsburg* (New York: Dey Street Publishers, 2015).

6. Patricia J. Williams, "Anita Hill's Second Act," *Harper's Bazaar*, October 1997.

7. John Updike, *The Early Stories: 1953–1975* (New York: Random House Trade Paperbacks, 2003), p. 597.

8. Charles Bukowski, *The Most Beautiful Woman in Town* (San Francisco: City Lights, 1967), p. 58.

9. Vladimir Nabokov, *Lolita* (New York: Random House, 1995), p. 1.

10. White, E. B. *Charlotte's Web* (New York, Harper & Brothers, 1952), p. 1.

how to make herself agreeable

1. Vladimir Nabokov, *Lolita* (New York: Random House, 1995), p. 316.

2. This conversation took place in 2007 when models earned a median hourly pay of $10.83 but today's numbers don't look much different. The most recent Department of Labor report listed median hourly wage for models at $15.34, or more than $10 less than what MIT's Living Wage Calculator estimates a single individual with no children will need to live in New York City. U.S. Bureau of Labor Statistics, https://www.bls.gov/ooh/sales/models.htm, accessed September 3, 2023. Living Wage Calculator, Amy K. Glasmeier and the Massachusetts Institute of Technology, https://livingwage.mit.edu.

3.   See, for example, the refusal of garment factory owners in Karnataka, India, to pay four hundred thousand workers in compliance with the region's April 2020 minimum wage increase resulting in $58 million in unpaid wages. Workersrights.org, https://www.workersrights.org/our-work/wage-theft-in-karnataka/, accessed September 3, 2023. Or the $40 billion in canceled orders at the start of the Covid-19 pandemic, many of which were completed and even shipped, that Remake's director of advocacy and policy Elizabeth L. Cline explained in *Atmos* in July of 2021 "[is] the equivalent salaries of Bangladesh's four million garment workers for the next eight years and the salaries and benefits of most of the world's 50 million garment workers for the rest of 2020." "The Power of #PayUp," *Atmos*, July 14, 2020, https://atmos.earth/payup-bangladesh-factory-worker-social-campaign/.

4.   In June 2020, 93 percent of 311 surveyed fashion brands were not paying a living wage to any of their suppliers, according to Fashion Checker, a website launched by the Clean Clothes Campaign and funded by the European Union, https://fashionchecker.org/, accessed September 3, 2023.

5.   Alan B. Krueger, "Rock and Roll, Economics, and Rebuilding the Middle Class," Whitehouse.gov, June 12, 2013, https://obamawhitehouse.archives.gov/blog/2013/06/12/rock-and-roll-economics-and-rebuilding-middle-class.

6.   "Men are 150 percent more likely to be the victims of violent crimes than women are. Men are more likely to be both victims and perpetrators of crimes. Men are more likely to be assaulted, injured, or killed when alcohol is involved. Men are more likely to be victimized by a stranger (63 percent of violent victimizations), whereas women are more likely to be victimized by someone they know (62 percent of violent victimizations). Women are more likely to be victimized in their home or in the home of someone they know, whereas men are more likely to be victimized in public. And yet it is women who are treated to 'suggestions' about how to protect themselves from public stranger assaults: go out with a friend, don't drink too much, don't walk home alone, take a self-defense class." Jaclyn Friedman and Jessica Valenti, *Yes Means Yes:*

Visions of Female Sexual Power and a World Without Rape (Berkeley: Seal Press, 2008), p. 23, citing Bureau of Justice statistics.

white cyc

1. Michelle Cliff, "Notes on Speechlessness," *Sinister Wisdom* 5 (1978): 5–9.
2. Rebecca Solnit, "How to Be a Writer: 10 Tips from Rebecca Solnit," Literary Hub, September 13, 2016.
3. Michelle Cliff, "A Journey into Speech," in *The Land of Look Behind* (Ithaca, N.Y.: Firebrand Books, 1985), p. 16.
4. Gisele Bündchen, *Lessons* (New York: Avery, 2018), p. 13.
5. Ashley Graham, *A New Model* (New York: Dey Street Books, 2017), p. 14.
6. Naomi Campbell, *Naomi* (New York: Universe, 1996), p. 28.
7. Dorian Leigh, *The Girl Who Had Everything* (New York: Bantam Books, 1980), p. 8.
8. Marilyn Monroe, *My Story* (1974; Kindle Edition, 2007), locs. 305–6 of 1456.
9. Iman, *I Am Iman* (New York: Universe, 2001), p. 58.
10. Waris Dirie, *Desert Flower* (New York: HarperCollins, 1998), p. 214.
11. Alek Wek, *Alek* (New York: HarperCollins, 2007), p. 194.

tableau vivant

1. Malcolm Daniel, "The Countess da Castiglione," metmuseum.org, July 2007, www.metmuseum.org/toah/hd/coca/hd_coca.htm.
2. Ibid.
3. Abigail Solomon-Godeau, "The Legs of the Countess," *October* 39 (1986): 65–108.
4. Sarah Boxer, "A Goddess of Self-Love Who Did Not Sit Quietly," *The New York Times,* October 13, 2000, www.nytimes.com/2000/10/13/arts/photography-review-a-goddess-of-self-love-who-did-not-sit-quietly.html.
5. Solomon-Godeau, "Legs of the Countess," p. 83.
6. Kelly D. Suschinsky and Martin L. Lalumière, "Prepared for Any-

thing? An Investigation of Female Genital Arousal in Response to Rape Cues," *Psychological Science* 22, no. 2 (2011): 159–65.

7. Nathalie Léger, *Exposition* (London, Les Fugitives, 2019), p. 7.

8. Emphasis mine. Pierre Apraxine and Xavier Demange, *La Divine Comtesse: Photographs of the Countess De Castiglione* (New Haven, Conn.: Yale University Press, 2000), p. 12.

9. Emphasis mine. Solomon-Godeau, "Legs of the Countess," p. 70.

10. In her dissertation "Performing Photographs: Memory, History, and Display" (Louisiana State University, 2008), Melanie Kitchen provides a careful analysis of two portraits and finds both make strong contemporary political and personal commentary. In one, she finds that Oldoini's portrayal of a heroine from a popular novel critiques France's postrevolution aristocracy; in the other, her dress references a kindred maligned aristocrat, Maria Luisa of Spain.

cheap, heavy earrings

1. Grace Jones, *I'll Never Write My Memoirs* (New York: Gallery Books, 2015), p. 108.

2. Kirstin Downey, *The Woman Behind the New Deal: The Life of Frances Perkins, FDR's Secretary of Labor and His Moral Conscience* (New York: Knopf Doubleday, 2009).

3. Rosalind Rosenberg, *Jane Crow: The Life of Pauli Murray* (New York, Oxford University Press, 2017).

4. Patricia Bell-Scott, *The Firebrand and the First Lady: Portrait of a Friendship; Pauli Murray, Eleanor Roosevelt, and the Struggle for Social Justice* (New York: Knopf, 2016).

5. Following the Pauli Murray Center's guidance, I refer to Murray as they/them here as I am describing their early life, https://www.paulimurraycenter.com/pronouns-pauli-murray.

6. Fernanda Bárcia de Mattos, Valeria Esquivel, David Kucera, and Sheba Tejani, "The State of the Apparel and Footwear Industry: Employment, Automation and Their Gender Dimensions," Background Paper Series of the Joint EU-ILO Project, January 2022.

7. Which I first learned from Anne Elizabeth Moore's 2016 book *Threadbare: Clothes, Sex, and Trafficking* (Portland, OR: Microcosm

Publishing, 2016), p. 113: "The garment industry . . . very rarely pays more than half a living wage (including to folks who work fast fashion retail in U.S. urban centers). This helps keep women in poverty around the globe." And is still unfortunately true in 2023 (see research from The Industry We Want, https://www .theindustrywewant.com/wages).

8. "Alan Kreuger . . . is one among many to point out that . . . high-inequality countries tend to be countries with low mobility, a relationship that led Krueger to suppose that, as income inequality is increasing in the U.S., so too mobility may be declining." Miles Corak, "Economic Mobility," in "State of the Union: The Poverty and Inequality Report 2016," special issue, *Pathways*, 2016, p. 52, https://inequality.stanford.edu/sites/default/files/Pathways-SOTU -2016-Economic-Mobility-3.pdf. "Even societies that are held to have 'high' mobility aren't all *that* mobile. . . . Sweden has one of the highest rates of social mobility in the world, but a 2012 study found that the top of the income spectrum is dominated by people whose parents were rich." James Surowiecki, "The Mobility Myth," *The New Yorker,* February 23, 2014, www.newyorker.com/magazine/2014 /03/03/the-mobility-myth.

9. "Bangladesh Factory Collapse Toll Passes 1,000," BBC.com, May 10, 2013.

10. Jim Yardley, "Report on Deadly Factory Collapse in Bangladesh Finds Widespread Blame," *The New York Times,* May 22, 2013.

11. Environmental Protection Agency, "Textiles: Material-Specific Data," updated December 3, 2022, www.epa.gov/facts-and-figures -about-materials-waste-and-recycling/textiles-material-specific-data.

12. In 2021 Al Jazeera reported thirty-nine thousand tons (or seventy-eight million pounds) of secondhand and unsold clothing are being dumped annually in Atacama Desert alone. "Chile's Desert Dumping Ground for Fast Fashion Leftovers," Al Jazeera, November 8, 2021, www.aljazeera.com/gallery/2021/11/8/chiles-desert-dumping -ground-for-fast-fashion-leftovers.

13. Mary Hanbury, "20 Companies Dominate the World's Fashion Industry. Here's Who Makes the List," *Insider,* December 9, 2018, www.businessinsider.com/nike-zara-tj-maxx-top-list-global-fashion

-brands-2018-12. An even smaller group owns the fashion media, and then there are those individuals who, like me, have at times, and with other options, supported them uncritically. We few, with a stranglehold on power-over, too often define, perhaps ignorantly, perhaps not, what is now the impact of the fashion industry.

14. Investigations by *The New York Times, The Wall Street Journal,* and *Axios* have found that major brands including H&M, Adidas, Lacoste, Ralph Lauren, Abercrombie, and PVH Corp. (including Calvin Klein and Tommy Hilfiger) are using slave labor in Uighur internment camps in China. They estimate that one fifth of all cotton yarn originates in the region. Elizabeth Paton and Austin Ramzy, "Coalition Brings Pressure to End Forced Uighur Labor," *The New York Times,* July 23, 2020, www.nytimes.com/2020/07/23/fashion/uighur-forced-labor-cotton-fashion.html?referringSource=articleShare.

15. Research by Stand.Earth found a hundred of the biggest brands, including Nike, Adidas, Louis Vuitton, and Gucci had supply chain links to leather producers with a recorded history of illegal deforestation, https://stand.earth/resources/nowhere-to-hide-how-the-fashion-industry-is-linked-to-amazon-rainforest-destruction/.

16. "Rethinking Business Models for a Thriving Fashion Industry," *How to Build a Circular Economy,* ellenmacarthurfoundation.org/fashion-business-models/overview, accessed August 28, 2023.

17. The Fabric Act, thefabricact.org/. Accessed 21 Oct. 2023.

18. "Wages in the global south at this time were so low (56 cents an hour in El Salvador in 1995, for example), apparel importers were often able to get their labor costs down to less than 1 percent of the retail price of their clothes." Elizabeth Cline, *Overdressed* (New York: Penguin, 2013), p. 53. Although it is very hard to find accurate data, the Clean Clothes Campaign's current estimate puts wages for production at about 3 percent of sale price, noting that this could be less for luxury fashion, whose workers rarely make more than those sewing for cheaper "fast fashion" brands (and often make less, see: 2019 report from the University of Sheffield, "Corporate Commitments to Living Wages in the Garment Industry," which found that "H&M and C&A were the only ones [of twenty large brands

surveyed] whose supplier codes of conduct reflected ACT's definition of a living wage in their compensation expectations").

19. Mohammad A. Razzaque, "Bangladesh: En Route to LDC Gradua-
tion: Firm-Level Preparedness in the Textile and Clothing Sector,"
https://www.un.org/development/desa/dpad/wp-content/uploads
/sites/45/Garment-Study-Bangladesh.pdf, 2021.

20. "Cambodia Economic Update: The Garment Sector in Perspective," World Bank Group, https://documents1.worldbank.org
/curated/en/575221480949830789/pdf/108982-WP-ENGLISH
-P148100-PUBLIC-FinalCEUOctoberEnglish.pdf, 2016.

21. Moore, *Threadbare*.

22. Maurya Wickstrom, *Performing Consumers: Global Capital and Its The-
atrical Seductions* (New York: Routledge, 2006), p. 27.

23. "Capitalism and racism . . . did not break from the old order but
rather evolved from it to produce a modern world system of 'racial
capitalism' dependent on slavery, violence, imperialism, and geno-
cide." Cedric Robinson, *Black Marxism* (Chapel Hill, N.C.: The University of North Carolina Press, 2000), p. xiii.

24. Michael Gross, *Model* (New York: William Morrow and Company,
1995), p. 25.

25. Guy Trebay, "Gisele Inc.," *The New York Times,* May 14, 2016, www
.nytimes.com/2016/05/15/fashion/gisele-bundchen-model
-supermodel.html.

26. Naomi Campbell, *Naomi* (New York: Universe, 1996), p. 21.

27. Minh-Ha T. Pham, "Stories the Fashion Media Won't Tell," *The Nation,* January 18, 2019.

redacted

1. Rebecca Walker, *To Be Real* (New York: Anchor Books, 1995), p. 215.

2. Michael Cohen, "How For-Profit Prisons Have Become the Biggest
Lobby No One Is Talking About," *The Washington Post,* April 28,
2015.

3. "Power-with is the psychological and social power gained through
collective resistance and struggle and through the creation of an al-

ternative set of narratives. It is relational and interactive. It requires participation. As the colleague we called Martha in Chapter 4 explained, 'Participation affords power even aside from direct results . . . [it offers] a chance for claiming dignity even at the moment that it is at risk of being denied.'" Lani Guinier and Gerald Torres, *The Miner's Canary: Enlisting Race, Resisting Power, Transforming Democracy* (Cambridge, Mass.: Harvard University Press, 2003), p. 141.

4. "White female racism undermines feminist struggle. As long as [this group] . . . or any group, defines liberation as gaining social equality with ruling-class white men, they have a vested interest in the continued exploitation and oppression of others." bell hooks, *Feminist Theory: From Margin to Center* (London: Pluto Press, 2000), p. 16.

5. Sarah Schulman, *Conflict Is Not Abuse* (Vancouver: Arsenal Pulp Press, 2016), p. 78.

6. Jodi Kantor and Rachel Abrams, "Gwyneth Paltrow, Angelina Jolie and Others Say Weinstein Harassed Them." *The New York Times,* October 10, 2017, www.nytimes.com/2017/10/10/us/gwyneth -paltrow-angelina-jolie-harvey-weinstein.html.

7. Maureen Dowd, "This Is Why Uma Thurman Is Angry," *The New York Times,* February 3, 2018, www.nytimes.com/2018/02/03 /opinion/sunday/this-is-why-uma-thurman-is-angry.html.

8. Janice Dickinson, *No Lifeguard on Duty* (New York: HarperCollins, 2002), p. 174.

9. Ibid., p. 226.

10. Carré Otis with Hugo Schwyzer, *Beauty, Disrupted* (New York: HarperCollins, 2011), p. 79.

11. Schulman, *Conflict,* p. 17.

12. Otis, *Beauty, Disrupted,* p. 81.

13. Anonymous, "Were You Raped by ████████?," *Medium,* Into the Raw, June 4, 2016, medium.com/into-the-raw/were-you-raped-by -g%C3%A9████████8ffb01a8de6c.

14. "'Everyone Knew', Models Denounce the Alleged Abuses of Their Agents Since the 1980s," Web24 News, January 19, 2020, web .archive.org/web/20200717004924/ https://www.web24.news/a/2020

/01/everyone-knew-models-denounce-the-alleged-abuses-of-their
-agents-since-the-1980s.html.

15. Lucy Osborne, Harry Davies, and Stephanie Kirchgaessner, "Teen
Models, Powerful Men and Private Dinners: When Trump Hosted
Look of the Year," *The Guardian,* March 14, 2020, www.theguardian
.com/us-news/2020/mar/14/teen-models-powerful-men-when-donald
-trump-hosted-look-of-the-year.

16. Tatiana the Anonymous Model, "Modeling and the Tragedy of
Karen Mulder," *Jezebel,* July 1, 2009.

17. Jill Dodd, *The Currency of Love* (New York: Atria/Enliven Books,
2017), p. 89.

18. Lucy Osborne, "'He Wanted to Control Me Completely': The
Models Who Accuse ███████ of Sexual Assault," *The Guardian,* October 17, 2020, www.theguardian.com/fashion/2020/oct/17
/he-wanted-to-control-me-completely-the-models-who-accuse
███████of-sexual-assault.

19. Otis, *Beauty, Disrupted,* p. 81.

20. Elizabeth Paton, Vanessa Friedman, and Constant Méheut, "Former
Fashion Models Accuse Top Agent of Rape and Sexual Assault,"
The New York Times, September 28, 2020, www.nytimes.com/2020
/09/28/world/europe/███████france-models-accusations.html
?smid=tw-share.

21. Ariella Aïsha Azoulay, *The Civil Contract of Photography* (Brooklyn,
N.Y.: Zone Books, 2008), p. 217.

22. Ibid., p. 217.

23. For her PhD thesis, psychologist Judith Grob of the University of
Groningen asked subjects to look at disgusting images while hiding
their emotions or while holding pens in their mouths to prevent
frowning. A control group reacted as they pleased. Subjects from
the first two groups reported feeling less disgusted afterward than
the control group. But when she administered a series of cognitive
tasks, subjects who had repressed their emotions performed poorly
on memory tasks and completed the word tasks to produce more
negative words—they completed "gr_ss" as "gross" rather than
"grass," for instance—compared with controls. Melinda Wenner,
"Smile! It Could Make You Happier," *Scientific American,* Septem-

ber 1, 2009, www.scientificamerican.com/article/smile-it-could-make
-you-happier/.

24. Tim V. Salomons et al., "Voluntary Facial Displays of Pain Increase
Suffering in Response to Nociceptive Stimulation," *Journal of Pain* 9,
no. 5 (May 2008): 443–48.

25. Maureen Orth, "Death by Design," *Vanity Fair,* January 8, 2014,
www.vanityfair.com/news/1996/09/claude-montana-wallis-franken.

26. Azoulay, *Civil Contract of Photography*, pp. 265–66.

27. Rucha Chitnis, "Garment Workers Organize to End Wage Theft,"
YES! Magazine, December 21, 2021, www.yesmagazine.org/social
-justice/2021/12/28/garment-workers-fashion-industry-wage-theft.

28. Edie Campbell, "Exclusive: Edie Campbell Pens Open Letter on
Model Abuse," *WWD,* November 9, 2017, wwd.com/feature/edie
-campbell-pens-open-letter-on-model-abuse-11044720/.

29. Ariella Aïsha Azoulay, *Civil Imagination* (London: Verso Books,
2012), p. 237.

quilt-making theory

1. Elizabeth Wissinger, *This Year's Model: Fashion, Media, and the Making of Glamour* (New York: NYU Press, 2015), p. 270.

2. Leon Stein, *Out of the Sweatshop: The Struggle for Industrial Democracy* (New York: Quadrangle/New Times Book Company, 1977),
p. 188.

3. Quoted in Mattie Kahn, *Young and Restless* (New York: Viking,
2023), p. 21.

4. "Sinead O`Connor—Arsenio Hall 1991," YouTube, May 4, 2011,
www.youtube.com/watch?v=mAf7fGEeRQs.

5. James Baldwin, *The Price of the Ticket: Collected Nonfiction: 1948–1985*
(Boston: Beacon Press, 1985), p. 310.

6. Mariame Kaba, "So You're Thinking About Becoming an Abolitionist," *Medium,* October 29, 2020.

7. Fred Moten, *Black and Blur* (Durham, N.C.: Duke University Press,
2017), p. 168.

about the author

CAMERON RUSSELL has spent the last twenty years working as a model for clients including Prada, Calvin Klein, Victoria's Secret, H&M, *Vogue,* and *Elle.* With over forty million views, she gave one of the top ten most popular TED talks on the power of image. She is the co-founder of Model Mafia, a collective of hundreds of fashion models striving for a more equitable, just, and sustainable industry, and was the force behind campaigns including #MyJobShouldNotIncludeAbuse, which brought the #MeToo movement to fashion. She continues organizing, consulting, and speaking, working to transform extractive supply chains and center climate justice. She lives in New York with her family.

about the type

This book was set in Dante, a typeface designed by Giovanni Mardersteig (1892–1977). Conceived as a private type for the Officina Bodoni in Verona, Italy, Dante was originally cut only for hand composition by Charles Malin, the famous Parisian punch cutter, between 1946 and 1952. Its first use was in an edition of Boccaccio's *Trattatello in laude di Dante* that appeared in 1954. The Monotype Corporation's version of Dante followed in 1957. Though modeled on the Aldine type used for Pietro Cardinal Bembo's treatise *De Aetna* in 1495, Dante is a thoroughly modern interpretation of that venerable face.